NEXT STEPS

Glorifying God With Joy
Through the Triumphs and Trials of Motherhood
with Biblical Hope

Trisha Ramos

Author of
Struggles and Sunshine

(I wanted to record this here for Eden Joy to enjoy reading one day when I'm no longer on this planet, these were all words from dear people that I ministered along side of in the effort to reach the Lost long before Eden was born)

"If you look up the word "diligent" in the dictionary, you will probably find the name "Trish." She is not only diligent, but she has a zeal for the lost, a good grip on biblical principles, and a deep and worshipful love for the God who gave her life. If I want something done quickly and done properly, I give it to Trish. I am honored to know her, and I thank God for the day she became involved in this ministry."

Ray Comfort
President/ Author/ T.V. Host
Living Waters Publications

"Every week on the radio with Trish is like opening up a Christmas present. You never know what you are going to get when she hits the streets. She is one of the boldest, most straight forward, refreshingly candid and yet clearly loving people I have ever heard witness to anyone. To get an idea, listen to petite Trish ask a linebacker from a college football team, "Are you fornicating?" Talk about courage! That is why every week is an adventure with Trish."

Todd Friel
Host
Wretched Radio / Formerly know as The Way of the Master Radio

"Having known Trisha for many years, I can confidently say that she is the real deal when it comes to living for the glory of God. She loves the Lord and the lost with a contagious passion. Her life is a living testimony of what it means to be a faithful ambassador for Christ."

Emeal Zwayne (E.Z.)
Vice President/ General Manager
Living Waters Publications

"We live in a culture of evangelistic cowardice, where the average Christian doesn't share the Gospel and often doesn't know the Gospel: Trish isn't the average Christian. With passion for Christ and genuine concern for others, Trish proclaims the whole counsel of God."

Adam P. Groza, Ph.D.
Vice President of Enrollment & Student Services
Golden Gate Baptist Theological Seminary

"Besides my wife, I don't know of another woman who encourages me to share my faith more than Trish."

Mark Spence
Dean of Students
The Biblical School of Evangelism

"In the summer of 2007, I had the special privilege of meeting Trish. I can tell you that she is every bit as personable, kind and genuine in person as she seems on the radio. She has a deep and abiding love of Jesus; a love which is beautifully manifested as she puts feet to her faith out in the highways and the hedges. Trish is both a blessing and a challenge to me and to all who know her. I thank and praise God for her faithful witness."

Justin Peters
Pastor of Evangelism
First Baptist Church, Vicksburg, MS

I totally enjoyed your book! I made a LOT of notes. On page 42 I had a "six little word" experience. One of the last times I broke down in Brandon's old disability van where the lift wouldn't work without the motor on and I was stuck in a hot van. We were at Home Depot in Sherman. Chris was at work in Plano-45 minute drive...so we sat waiting. A little elderly lady came over and saw the situation and asked "How can I help?" After she left, I just started to sob. AMAZING what a few kind words can do! So much so that I still talk about it to this day! So thankful you wrote this book! I have been encouraged greatly! Even through the difficulties of life, we have the greatest hope of all in the person of Jesus Christ! May we exalt His name forevermore!

Tina Maya
Mom to Brandon Maya
(brain aneurysm survivor and friend of Ray Comfort)

"I love every word."

Marissa, Mother of two, Frisco, TX

"This book is full of sweetness. Trish writes like she is talking to the reader."

JoAnn, Mother of two, McKinney, TX

"It is with great pleasure that I recommend my wife's book as a place where people can be infected with a passion to spread the gospel of Jesus Christ, and glorify God as a mom in daily life. My wife continues to be an example to me of why we exist, to know God and make Him known."

Emilio Ramos (Papa to Eden Joy)
Pastor for Preaching
Heritage Grace Community Church, Frisco, TX

ISBN: 978-0-9985939-2-0

First Edition

Cover design: Chafi Charneco

Interior layout: John Manning

⌘ PREFACE ⌘

"Why are you in despair, O my soul? And why are you disturbed within me? Hope in God, for I shall again praise Him, The help of my countenance and my God."

⟹Psalm 43:5

If you have not read my first book *Struggles and Sunshine* I recommend you grab a copy. The testimonies that I have received from numerous ladies is that they finished the book in 48 hours or less. A friend "Lauren" in California said she stayed up very late into the night because she couldn't put it down and woke up the next morning thinking about finishing it. It's where the story starts and *Next Steps* is a continuation of the first book. But with that said, you can certainly start on page one of this book and read through it especially since I wrote it in an easy-to-read journal style. That's what *Next Steps* is. It is a personal journal of prayers and reflections and insights from the Bible and it also includes wonderful memories of us raising Eden Joy, our only child. It's a real look into the life of one mom. The good, the bad, and the not so pretty. The days that are full of joy and the days that are full of aches and pains. Many of my words I pray will comfort mom's that are in a similar position and that battle the grief (at times) of their children growing. This book hopefully will also encourage your soul during the times that you might despair and feel as if you have failed your children. I understand the battle of despair and grief and have encountered the long days when the waves of grief come over me out of nowhere and the hollow, nagging pit in my stomach won't lift. If you've been there (or if you ARE there), then perhaps this book will help carry you just a bit along the way. After all, it is during these seasons and moments when we must wage war and dig into God's Word to lift our heads and our souls. As the psalmist said, "Why are you so downcast Oh my soul, hope in God, I will again praise Him." (Psalm 43:5). My prayer is that as you read daily with me through the pages, the insights and words that I have knit together with precious Scripture, to lighten your load and leave you with a hop in your step. Onward Christian Mothers!

For of Him, and through Him, and to Him, are all things. To Him be the glory forever. Amen.

December 14, 2019 (Eden's 3rd Birthday)
Trisha Nicole Ramos

⤜∘ CUDDLE ∘⤛

"If you then, being evil, know how to give good gifts to your children, how much more will your Father who is in heaven give what is good to those who ask Him!

⤜Matthew 7:11

*A*pril 25, 2019

I made a funny prayer request to God tonight, and I meant every word. The prayer stemmed from the day my friend, Tonia, told me about her trips home to visit her dear mom. She said that the two of them watched movies in bed and cuddled, just like they used to do when she was a child. That thought has stuck with me to this day, and tonight it came to mind when I was hanging blackout curtains in our bedroom. I thought, "I hope Eden is like that. Why don't I pray for it? 'Lord, if you would be willing, make Eden into a cuddle bug and endearing to me all her days. And, for my readers, grant their children (whatever age they are) a true love for You and their parents. Amen.'"

"If you then, being evil, know how to give good gifts to your children, how much more will your Father who is in heaven give what is good to those who ask Him!

⤜Matthew 7:11

⟋ MODESTY ⟍

"My soul, wait in silence for God only, For my hope is from Him."

⟹Psalm 62:5

*M*ay 2, 2019

Before bed, Eden and I read a most adorable book about the Gospel. On several pages, the little cartoon toddler girl reaches up and points to the heavens, inadvertently revealing her belly button. This accidental belly button reveal distracts Eden so much that I don't think she hears the true message of the book. Over and over, she says, "Little girl...can you pull your shirt down? We don't show our belly buttons."

I love her heart in this. May she grow to be a modest, godly woman who fears the Lord and hates evil. Lord, let it be said of us and our daughters that we are different than the culture. That we honor and fear You with our clothing and that our hearts and our clothes will bring honor to You. Amen.

"My soul, wait in silence for God only, For my hope is from Him."

⟹Psalm 62:5

❧ OFFERING ❧

"The LORD is my strength and my shield; My heart trusts in Him, and I am helped; Therefore my heart exults, And with my song I shall thank Him."

⟩Psalm 28:7

*M*ay 5, 2019

I did a bit of cleaning while Eden slept this morning. I found a gift bag I was going to put in our spare room along with all the other gift bags. I have a habit of saving them and re-gifting them. As I picked up this particular gift bag, it felt heavy, which was strange as I expected it to be empty. I looked inside and found a sweet potato wrapped in a paper towel and remembered that Eden had brought it to me the night before and said, "Mama, here's a gift for you." Thinking about it brings tears to my eyes. I don't want ever to get rid of the bag or the potato! What a sweet, sweet (potato) gift.

What sort of sweet offering can we give to God today? Perhaps a thankful attitude (even when it's hard). Or serving someone in some way (for His glory), or filling your home with worship. Whatever the wrapping your gift comes in today, let's aim to make our praise beautiful.

Tonight before bed, Eden said, "Mama, I was missing you today."

"What do you mean?" I asked. "When did you miss me?"

She said, "At church in the nursery."

I laughed because I was in the nursery with her the whole

time. It touched my heart to think maybe she just wanted to take me away from all the other children and have me by herself, much like the Lord when He would escape away to pray and spend time alone with the Father. I remember feeling this way towards my own mom when I was young. Wanting to just be with her. How special the mother and daughter relationship is. Thank you Lord that this is all just a picture of heaven and that in heaven we will have the ultimate union and relationship with You, Lord, and our communion with other believers will not have to end. What a joy. And perhaps each day you will reveal to us sweet sweet gifts that are sweeter than a sweet potato when we are in heaven with You. Amen.

"The LORD is my strength and my shield; My heart trusts in Him, and I am helped; Therefore my heart exults, And with my song I shall thank Him."

≈Psalm 28:7

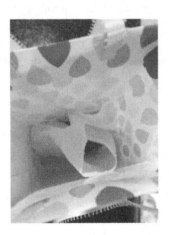 

"Blessed is the man who does not walk in the counsel of the wicked, or set foot on the path of sinners, or sit in the seat of mockers."

Psalm 1:1

*M*ay 7, 2019

Today, the song *Be Still My Soul* a very old song written back in 1752 by a lady named Katharina von Schlegel, ministered to me. Eden was sick two weeks ago, and I seem to be suffering with whatever she had. I have a lingering cough that tickles my throat and causes me to cough every few minutes. It's driving me batty, so when I stumbled upon the song, the lyrics were beautiful to my soul.

Be still, my soul: the Lord is on your side.
Bear patiently the cross of grief or pain;
leave to your God to order and provide;
in every change God faithful will remain.
Be still, my soul: your best, your heavenly friend
through thorny ways leads to a joyful end.

Be still, my soul: your God will undertake
to guide the future, as in ages past.
Your hope, your confidence let nothing shake;
all now mysterious shall be bright at last.
Be still, my soul: the waves and winds still know
the Christ who ruled them while he dwelt below.

Be still, my soul: the hour is hastening on
when we shall be forever with the Lord,
when disappointment, grief, and fear are gone,
sorrow forgot, love's purest joys restored.
Be still, my soul: when change and tears are past,
all safe and blessed we shall meet at last.

Despite the cough, I still had a lovely day with Eden. We ran errands and sang the words to Psalm 1 to a tune I made up and recorded on my phone. It's perfect for playing while we wait in traffic. I brought along some broccoli for the car ride too, and when the Psalmist says the righteous man, "will be like a tree planted by rivers of water and whatever he does will prosper," I reach back and hand Eden a broccoli "tree" to eat. She asked for me to play the song over and over, and for a "tree" too. I pray this tune sticks with her all her life.

If you would like to take up memorizing the Bible more intentionally (perhaps a paragraph or stanza or even a chapter at a time), I have learned through the years a few proven tips on memorization that have worked wonders for my slow brain:

1. The faster the tune, the better for memorizing. Slow songs tend to take longer to stick in your head.

2. Make the tune catchy or silly or fun; variations are better than monotone. For example, I've memorized Romans 8 before Eden was born and I made up about 8 different tunes to help me with memorizing the chapter. I sing the chapter through the house now and in the car and Eden is picking up a lot of it.

3. Listen to and/or sing your song throughout the day to learn it fast. And if you do this in the AM and the PM it will help to have songs of scripture as the last thing you hear before sleeping.

4. It's also beneficial for the recording to be in your voice. This tip I learned from Chad, my Navy Seal friend, who did this very thing to memorize different tactical plans. And since as Christians we are in a spiritual war,

I say grab your phone's voice recorder, hit record, and start singing.

My husband told me yesterday that many Muslim children memorize the entire Koran by the age of five. Did you know that the Koran is the size of the New Testament? To hear this was convicting to me as an adult. Why not start with a verse today, then go from there? Just chew on a verse that will minister to your heart and move to the next one. Our hearts always need the medicine of the Word, and Psalm 1 is a perfect place to start.

"Blessed is the man who does not walk in the counsel of the wicked, or set foot on the path of sinners, or sit in the seat of mockers."

—Psalm 1:1

⋙ ADOPTION ⋘

*M*ay 8, 2019

I had a bit of loneliness overcome my heart tonight. I've
been dreading the day my mom is no longer on this planet.
She left our home tonight after a lovely time at bible study
and talking and playing with Eden. And now I'm left with a
sense of deep sadness that life will not be the same in any way
when she goes to be with the Lord. Just the fact that no one
on the planet loves me as she does will be a big hit to my needy
heart (because whoever stops needing their mom?).

Romans 8 reminds us that "all creation groans" and we are
"eagerly waiting for our adoption as sons." What a thought.
We groan, and we mourn, sometimes even when nothing is
wrong. We know that this life is not all there is. We are waiting, and we know what we are waiting for has not yet come.

My mom was adopted when she was five years old. Her
mom died of cancer at 39 (the age I had Eden), so she never
really knew her. All she remembers is a blue robe she wore.
Interestingly enough, there is an old black and white photo
of my mom with her small family just days before her mom
died, and she is wearing a robe that I assume is the same one.
My mom's uncle adopted her after her mom passed. They took

care of her by ensuring her basic needs were met. She was given a pair of shoes twice a year; one black pair and one white pair that were to last all year long. Just writing that makes me cry. She had only a few outfits as well.

Along with minimal shoes and clothes, and because it was not a Christian home the love of the Lord was not present. The whole family went to a Catholic church almost weekly but was dead religiously. All of this reminded me of how different our adoption in Christ is. He takes us in and gives us everything! He gives Himself and His Kingdom, where we will rule and reign (and who are we to rule and reign over anything?).

There are five heavenly crowns mentioned in the New Testament that will be awarded to Believers as well, which is more than the number of shoes my mom had. They are:

1. The imperishable crown
2. The crown of rejoicing
3. The crown of righteousness
4. The crown of glory
5. The crown of life.

Paul's passage in 1 Corinthians 9:24-25 best defines for us how these crowns will be awarded. Maybe take a moment today and read that portion of Scripture. There is so much for us to look forward to. And just think Who is waiting to bring your adoption to competition, the glorious King of Kings!

"Seeing that His divine power has granted to us everything pertaining to life and godliness, through the true knowledge of Him who called us by His own glory and excellence."
—2 Peter 1:3

∼◎ COMMIT ◎∼

*M*ay 10, 2019

Today I remembered I hadn't wrote about one of our first trips to the Frisco Public Library (or as Eden calls it the Libraria). I had no idea what I was doing and what to look for, so I prayed, "Lord, lead me to books Eden will love." Shortly after the prayer, I found *Tiny: The Birthday Dog.* It looked like an adorable book with a dog on the cover that was huge but his name was Tiny. I took it home, opened it up, and had to pick my jaw up off the floor after I read the beautiful dedication from Rich Davis the illustrator of all Tiny Series books:

"To Jesus Christ, the One who lives in me and creates through me…to Him be all the glory."

How kind of the Lord to do this. I am certain if you are reading this you are a busy mom that has different projects or to-do lists or workloads or errands that you need to tackle. Let's commit our way to the Lord today and we have His Word on it that He WILL direct our path. Proverbs 3:6.

Let's cast our cares on Him today. We have His Word on it that He WILL sustain us. Psalm 55:22.

Today if you are needy and faint and weary, we have His Word that he WILL give power to the faint and increase the strength of the weak. Isa 40:29

Today if you are fearful, then look to His Word that says, "Do not fear for God is with you, do not be dismayed for I (God) am your God. I (God) will strengthen you and help you: I (God) will uphold you with my righteous right hand." Isaiah 41:10

What a hope we have. What a source of strength we have. What a Rock we have. Psalm 18:2

"So that in all things God may be glorified through Jesus Christ, to whom belongs the glory and dominion forever and ever. Amen."
1 Peter 4:11

⤜ TRACTS ⤛

"…making the most of your time, because the days are evil."
⤛Ephesians 5:16

*M*ay 11, 2019

Ran a few errands today, and made sure I had a lot of tracts in my bag before I left. I knew it would be busy out. Saturdays always are.

At our first stop, a lady came up to Eden sitting in the shopping cart and said, "Hi." Eden said, "Hi" back. The lady said she had three boys of her own, six grandkids and one great-grandchild. Eden was sweet to her and handed her a gospel tract from Ray Comfort's ministry. She was touched and gladly took the tract.

Then we ran into Ross where I found a pair of sneakers to replace the ones I've had for four years, and Eden found a stuffed sheep that was half her size for just a few dollars. I had to get it. We headed to the check out where it seems everyone else had the same idea. I decided to redeem the time and pass out a gospel tract to everyone in line. I said, "Here's a gift for you. Maybe reading it will make the line go faster." It was nice to see people chuckle at that. And, amazingly, the line did move very fast. One person even got out of line, which was an answer to prayer. The next time you find yourself in a long line, say a prayer, and try passing out tracts and see what happens.

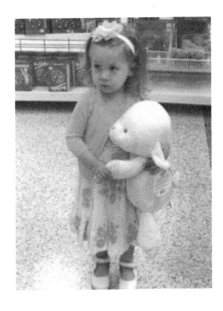

MODEL

"Strength and honor are her clothing, and she can laugh at the days to come."

—Proverbs 31:25

May 12, 2019

Eden prayed this today: "Thank you, Lord, for Mama's nose and Mama's eyes. Thank you for the rain and the sun. I just pray we won't get any coughs." This made me chuckle. I don't think anyone but me has ever prayed for my big Italian nose. I've prayed for my nose to be somehow smaller, but God bless Eden's childlike heart that she doesn't care about things like that.

Perhaps today we can thank God for our noses and all the faculties that He's given us. And, just maybe today, we can aim to use our senses for God's glory and His kingdom.

Lord, we thank you for our Moms who cared for us and used all of their means to do so. Thank you, Lord, for the Proverbs 31 Woman whose children rose up and called her "blessed." Help us to model her hard work and caring heart. In Christ's name, amen.

"Strength and honor are her clothing, and she can laugh at the days to come."

=Proverbs 31:25

"…speaking to one another in psalms and hymns and spiritual songs, singing and making melody in your heart to the Lord,"

⇒Ephesians 5:19

*M*ay 17, 2019

I limit my time greatly on my phone, and especially on Facebook. I know how much of a time-waster it can be. And if I am on Facebook I try to make it meaningful or to take something away that will encourage my soul. Tonight I saw on my Facebook newsfeed a beautiful picture of some friends in California with their five children. Some of you may know Mark Spence from Ray Comfort's ministry. He wrote a meaningful tribute to his five children (who I believe all profess to know the Lord). Mark and his wife Laura are dear friends of ours and have been great examples of what it means to persevere and raise a godly family in this dark world. Here's what he wrote:

> *"Humbled that the Lord would overflow my life with these gracious gifts. I am loved richly by them, and I give God thanks for how they love and care for me. I know they ultimately belong to God before me. They were created by Him and for His Glory. They were created for the purpose of knowing God and pointing others to the mercy, grace, faithfulness, and greatness of our God. They have a living hope because Christ stood in their place and satisfied the wrath the Father righteously had toward their sin. He took the punishment for us. Jesus Christ is victor and rose from the dead! He conquered the grave. May my children desire to always live for His will above their own. May they cherish the truth of Scripture and stand upon it as their constant firm foundation. May Christ always be sweeter*

to them than anything this world has to offer. This song below is often being sung in our home. May these lyrics forever be the theme of our hearts.

Should nothing of our efforts stand
No legacy survive
Unless the Lord does raise the house
In vain its builders strive
To you who boast tomorrow's gain
Tell me what is your life?
A mist that vanishes at dawn
All glory be to Christ!
All glory be to Christ our king!
All glory be to Christ!
His rule and reign will ever sing
All glory be to Christ!
His will be done His kingdom come On earth as is above
Who is Himself our daily bread
Praise Him the Lord of love
Let living water satisfy
The thirsty without price
We'll take a cup of kindness yet
All glory be to Christ!
All glory be to Christ our king! All glory be to Christ!
His rule and reign will ever sing
All glory be to Christ!
When on the day the great I Am
The faithful and the true
The Lamb who was for sinners slain
Is making all things new
Behold our God shall live with us
And be our steadfast light
And we shall ere his people be
All glory be to Christ!
All glory be to Christ our king! All glory be to Christ!
His rule and reign will ever sing
All glory be to Christ!"

We sing this song often during our family devotions with Eden. What a powerful song with such rich truth. Perhaps we can all have this tune on our lips today. Sing Praise!

"…speaking to one another in psalms and hymns and spiritual songs, singing and making melody in your heart to the Lord,"

Ephesians 5:19

⟨⟩ HONOR ⟨⟩

"And we know that God causes all things to work together for good to those who love God, to those who are called according to His purpose."

≈Romans 8:28

*M*ay 18, 2019

I am trying to find ways to make our home run more efficiently and save money. I decided to remove the solar lights in our back yard, which didn't work well, and return them to Costco for a $50 refund. But Emilio told me the night before to leave them because "they put out a little light."

However, he didn't know that I had already texted the lawn man to remove them. I decided that it wouldn't be a big deal to have them taken down and that he wouldn't mind and would understand when I explained to him what happened because after all in my mind I was "helping" our family and I am supposed to be a helpmate.

Yesterday, I saw the lawn man in our backyard and he had done what I asked. The lights were on our back porch, so I grabbed a big white bag from The Container Store that I had in the garage, threw the lights in there, opened the back of our SUV and tossed it for my next trip to Costco.

Today, Emilio, Eden and I were driving in our SUV to our friend's home for a lovely dinner, when I noticed a big red ant right next to my leg, then another, and another. The car seemed infested, and I almost felt like we were in Egypt during the plagues. There were so many ants that Emilio decided to pull off to the side of the road after which he found the source of the problem: the lights in the bag were filled with red ants!

Poor Emilio must have killed 100 of them in under five minutes.

I told him that it was all my fault; I should have listened to him and texted the lawn guy right away instructing him not to take them down (even though it would have been at midnight hahaha). He was so sweet about it, never once saying anything harsh. What a lesson I will always remember.

Let's aim today to honor our husbands by obeying in the "little" things so that we don't have an infestation of little things in our lives.

By the way, the lights are now in the trash. There went the $50. God's ways are (always) higher than mine.

"And we know that God causes all things to work together for good to those who love God, to those who are called according to His purpose."

—Romans 8:28

MAGNITUDE

"Then God made two great lights: the greater light to rule the day, and the lesser light to rule the night. He made the stars also."

⇒Genesis 1:16

May 22, 2019

From Ray Comfort's Evidence Bible:

Make sure you don't miss the magnitude of what God accomplished in creating the sun. Its surface temperature is about 10,000 degrees Fahrenheit, with the temperature at the core around 27 million degrees Fahrenheit. That's hot. The sun's diameter is about 870,000 miles (109 times greater than Earth), and it is 333,000 times heavier—and that is only one of over 100 billion stars that God made. It burns an incredible seven million tons of natural gas every second. And Almighty God spoke it into existence.

"Then God made two great lights: the greater light to rule the day, and the lesser light to rule the night. He made the stars also."

⇒Genesis 1:16

HANDIWORK

"The earth is the LORD's, and the fullness thereof, the world and all who dwell therein."

—Psalm 24:1

May 24, 2019

Today was special. Eden put on the headset Emilio uses for open-air preaching and asked to have it turned on. She then, unprompted, started quoting Genesis 1:1-5. What a treat it was to listen to her speak about God speaking things into existence. Then, before naptime, she pretended she was talking to Jesus on the phone and wanted to know if He had a computer. I don't know what His answer was.

If you think about it, both of those things required the use of her ears, which I believe I have discovered the reason why God designed them in such a funny way. I mean, just look at the ear, isn't it bizarre looking? And babies are so fascinated with them. I don't believe there has been a day when Eden has not played with my ears before going to sleep. Giving me a good ear massage must really help her to fine tune her motor skills. I think I remember doing the same thing for my mom.

And isn't it remarkable where God placed the ears? He put them in just the right spot for us to talk to our little ones as we carry them around town, instructing them discreetly about everything we see. God is such a genius. What an awesome Creator we have.

Thank you, Lord, for opening our eyes to You and for allowing us to see Your handiwork and fingerprints everywhere. After all, the earth is Yours and all it contains!

"The earth is the LORD's, and the fullness thereof, the world and all who dwell therein."

 ⸗Psalm 24:1

⟨⟩ BIGGER ⟨⟩

*Wait on the Lord; Be of good courage, And He shall strengthen
your heart; Wait, I say, on the Lord!*

Psalm 27:14

June 2, 2019

Eden is napping in my arms as we sit outside of Whole-
foods in Newport Beach, California in our rental car.

After a wonderful ladies' tea hosted by our church yesterday, we left DFW airport with a direct flight to Santa
Ana.

Our flight started a bit slow as we taxied onto the run-
way and sat for an hour and thirty minutes waiting for a
storm to pass before take off. But it was not too trouble-
some because I meditated on God's faithfulness and how
he provided a wonderful encounter at the luggage check-in
counter.

The young man behind the counter commented on my
shirt that says "Salvation" on the front saying, "That is the
best shirt in the world!" He had so much joy in his voice
and eyes. He told us he kept his bible on his desk. I gave
him tracts, to which he was truly grateful. He continued
with his work, charging us for our overweight, and giant,
bag. Emilio decided that we would take one piece of luggage this trip and put everything in it. Typically, I don't like
checking bags at the airport, opting instead to pack light
and bring a carry-on. But this time the plan sounded fine.

Eden was thrilled to watch the bags going on the conveyer belt and watched as the little man picked up our big bag, put it on the belt, and off it went.

And off we went; however, when we arrived in California, our luggage did not.

As I think back, it seemed the baggage guy was so excited about the Lord that he got distracted and never tagged our luggage. We called the airport today, but they could not find it. We also filed a claim, giving the link to UnpopularTheMovie.com to people on the other end of the line.

What struck me funny is our message from yesterday's ladies' tea was all on God taking care of the birds, and how He will care for His children (Matt 6:26).

At the airport in California, while we were scrambling trying to locate our one piece of luggage, Eden had spotted a little girl with a blue cat. And she said out loud, "Mama, may I please go over and say hello to that blue cat?" Some people overheard her and "oohed" and "aahed," so I gave them gospel tracts as well and thanked them for delighting in her.

Eden didn't have a care in the world as we were searching and searching for the missing bag. Her care was important to her, though. She just wanted to find that blue cat again. I knew where it was, though. She couldn't see it but I could, because I was taller. I was able to see it from my point of view. Just like Eden, I'm too small to find our missing bag, but God is bigger and is all-seeing. He knows the exact location of it even as I write this. And same for you, dear reader, is there someone Lost in your life? God is able to find them and save them (Luke 15:4-5). Is there something troubling you that you don't have an answer to? God can help bring comfort to your heart as you wait on Him in patience (Psalm 27:14) and He will strengthen your heart.

Lord, we will wait on you to see what Your great hand does with the cares in our life. They are always big to us but not to

You. Thank you that you are bigger and wiser than any of our foes or any of the trials that face us today. Amen.

Eden on the airplane enjoying snacks before the luggage problem.

⤙ GIFTS ⤚

"Thanks be to God for His indescribable gift!"

⤙ 2 Corinthians 9:15

*J*une 6, 2019

We are in California on vacation, so Eden and I walked to a few local stores today while Emilio went fishing. One was a giant candy store where I told her she could choose one thing from the whole store. After examining all the candy, she decided on the smallest tootsie pop she could find. I wanted to buy her a yummy looking cake with sprinkles, but she was settled on her find.

It was surprising that Eden didn't choose something grander seeing that I let her pick from anything in the sea of chocolates and candies. It reminded me of Solomon when God said He would give him anything he wanted. All that Solomon had to do was ask, and instead of lofty things, he chose wisdom. It's not even tangible, but its effects are far-reaching.

I ended up loving Eden's wisdom, and so did my wallet; I spent a whopping 20 cents.

After the candy store, we went next door to a coffee shop called Reborn, where I ordered a rare treat (since I hardly go to coffee shops), a small decaf almond milk coffee, and gave the staff gospel tracts. A few minutes, later I heard a staff member say, "Would she like one of these cookies for free?" She motioned to the whole front counter filled with fresh bags of cookies. They were beautiful, with the exact sprinkles as the cake at the last store that I was dreaming of for Eden. What a gift of kindness from the Lord.

Then we walked a couple of doors down to a health food cafe called Jan's Health Bar just to look at the menu. They had terrific healthy smoothies, which I try to make at home daily. I gave the workers tracts and didn't buy anything, but said I'd be back. Eden and I enjoyed their cute cafe for a bit and gazed out the clean windows at the beautiful California weather. Minutes later, one of the workers asked if we would like a smoothie. Someone ordered a wrong one by mistake, and I'm glad they did as it was delicious.

Before bed, Eden said some very kind things such as, "I like to shop with you, Mama, and I like to color with you, and I like to go upstairs with you." And I thought to myself, "We don't have any stairs," but then remembered the stairs at the beach that take you to the water. I must say I love all those things too.

Thank you, Lord, for giving us the ultimate stairway to heaven, through Jesus Christ. Thank you for the dream Jacob had of the angels descending up and down on a ladder, which is a picture of Jesus, that He is our access to heaven. Thank you, Lord, that You bridged the gap with the cross from Earth to Heaven so that we can cross safely to meet you when we die. Thank you, Lord, that in You we have been made complete (Col 2:10). Thank you that You are the head of all principality and power (Col 2:10). And thank you that on the cross you "disarmed the rulers and authorities and made a public spectacle of them, having triumphed over them (Col 2:15). Amen.

"Thanks be to God for His indescribable gift!"

≈2 Corinthians 9:15

⚮ OVERWHELMED ⚮

June 7, 2019

I received a sweet text from one of the ladies in our church who is reading my first book, *Struggles and Sunshine*:

"I've been reading your book for the last hour. The chapter titled "Next" has me weeping. I can't even describe what emotions you have stirred up inside me! I need time to retreat and continue weeping. When you have a full house, it can be challenging, to say the least.

I have tried my best to live my life by Elisabeth Elliot's wise words of just doing the next thing. Every now and then, I lose focus and find myself overwhelmed and become undone, but God reminds me somehow (like He just did with this chapter) and I get back on track, continuing the race with my eyes fixed on Him, and I'm ready to do the next thing. Love you, sis!"

When life gets overwhelming, do the next thing, beloved reader. Our to-do lists may be long, but not near as long as Noah's in his day. Can you imagine all he and his wife had to do in the ark? Talk about a full house!

"The LORD your God is in your midst, A victorious warrior. He will exult over you with joy, He will be quiet in His love, He will rejoice over you with shouts of joy."

⟨Zephaniah 3:17

❧ REJOICE ❧

*"Enter His gates with thanksgiving
And His courts with praise.
Give thanks to Him, bless His name."*

⟩Psalm 100:4

*J*une 8, 2019

Our luggage has been found! I feel as if I found my lost sheep. And you know what's funny. Eden had a lost sheep that was in the luggage and now it's been found! Glory to God.

I'm thankful for praying friends, especially my mom, who labored in prayer, and JoAnn, who spent countless hours going through every bag in two terminals at DFW Airport.

If we rejoiced over luggage can you imagine how much more the angels rejoice over one lost soul that is found (Luke 15:8-10)?!

Upon hearing our luggage was found, Eden said, "Praise the Lord!" A big "amen" to that.

"Enter His gates with thanksgiving
And His courts with praise.
Give thanks to Him, bless His name."

≡Psalm 100:4

"Whatever you do in word or deed, do all in the name of the Lord Jesus, giving thanks through Him to God the Father."

⟲Colossians 3:17

June 9, 2019

Today we went for a walk at the beach. Eden and I stood on a hill overlooking the ocean, and a dear older gentleman yelled out, "Great shirt!" I looked around to see who he was talking to when he said, "No, you! Great shirt about the Lord. Where did you get it?"

It's funny, but this simple shirt has created great responses that I would never have imagined. The front says "SALVA-TION" with the "T" being a cross, and the sleeve has "3:16". I'm so encouraged when I wear it that I think I need to buy another one.

""Whatever you do in word or deed, do all in the name of the Lord Jesus, giving thanks through Him to God the Father."

⟲Colossians 3:17

✎ CONVERSATIONS ✐

"Deal bountifully with Your servant that I may live and keep
Your Word."

➤Psalm 119:17

*J*une 10, 2019

Went to get my toes done at a small hole-in-the-wall nail salon in Corona Del Mar, California. The location could not have been better. The door was open so that the cool ocean breeze wafted inside overpowering the usual toxic nail polish fumes. As the pedicure lady took my foot out of the water, she said, "How long since you got your toes done?" I said, "It's been about a year." She said, "I can tell." I laughed.

The lady sitting next to me started chit-chatting and it turns out that she lives just minutes from where I live in Texas. Then we got on the topic of the Lord, and she said she was on her way to a For King and Country concert in Ontario, CA, which is the city where I grew up. I told her about my book, Struggles and Sunshine, and how it was available on Amazon. She took out her phone, and with a couple of clicks, she showed me she had bought it. What a blessing. Perhaps I should get my toes done more often. It literally pays off.

When we got "home" from the nail salon, the house keeper, for the home we were staying at, was there tidying up. The lady seemed to have a great joy about cleaning and a light in her eyes. I thought, "Maybe it's because they pay her well. Or because she lives by the beach."

Eden wanted to know her name. She said, "Susie." We also found out that she had three children and one grandchild. I asked if she went to church, and she said, "Yes, to big Calvary Chapel." I said, "Oh the late Chuck Smith's church. He baptized my husband right here in Corona Del Mar in the late '90s." She seemed touch by that fact, and then again when I gave her a copy of my book.

Thank you, Lord, for such conversations that encourage, and for the Gospel that gives us meaning and purpose and light. Amen.

Random thought tonight:

Since December 30, 2017, I've kept a particularly special text message on my phone. It came at a time when I was very ill because of my thyroid condition and was despairing of life. Eden had just turned one year old when I began battling severe nausea, a high heart rate, and some other scary symptoms. I thought one night while nursing Eden I was going to die and I called 911. My heart rate and blood pressure was through the roof and at stroke levels. But every time I called my thyroid doctor they kept assuring me that my medicine was appropriate and that I should even raise the dosage I was taking. That didn't seem correct to me based on how I felt. However, my blood work indicated otherwise, hence the doctor's recommendation.

Looking back, now I know the dosage was too high and I had to lower it on my own. My blood work had been skewed because of having to go to the bathroom too much (sorry for all the information but maybe it will help one of you that battle this). Throwing up will skew blood work also, so I learned to rely more on my symptoms than lab work when determining the correct dosage of medicine.

But back to December 30. The night before I received the text, I was meditating on Isaiah 49:30, which talks about God blessing His people so much that there will not be enough room in their homes. They will say, "move over" we are "too cramped here," which made me think about twins being cramped in the womb and my desire to have a set of them. I laughed out loud that God would ever give me twins seeing that at the time of the text, I was around 40 years old, but I committed the thought to the Lord nonetheless. About ten hours later (and still terribly ill), I received a text message from a long-distance friend of mine that texts me only about once a year. She said,

"Hi Trish, verse of the day from Psalm 119, I thought of you and then, Eden Joy. I was thinking if you were to have a set of male twins, you could name them Paradise. Get it? Pair-o-dise. 1&2! Yuk-yuk

I had told her in the past that I had memorized all of Psalm 119 and I was teaching it to Eden so when she was reading the verse of the day it must have reminded her of us.

I remember exactly where I was sitting when I received her text...on my living room floor with Eden playing in front of me. I laughed again and told Eden what had happened.

Now Eden often prays (sometimes daily) for twins for me and says she will name them "Ellie and Evan." Only God knows what will happen, but the name Evan is short for evangelism. I like that.

I also like the name Ezra. It's different but it's biblical and it's four letters like Eden. I like the name Adam too. I think it would go cute with Eden (Adam and Eden). And the next child could be named Flower (just kidding though that is cute too).

"Deal bountifully with Your servant that I may live and keep Your Word."

⇐Psalm 119:17

"And why are you worried about clothing? Observe how the lilies of the field grow; they do not toil nor do they spin."

Matthew 6:28

*J*une 11, 2019

We are supposed to go to Disneyland tomorrow to what they call "The happiest place on earth." Today wasn't so happy, though. It was rather hard.

Eden was fussy about many things and content with nothing. We went out to a nice lunch, walked a lot, got a treat, went to a toy store, walked by the ocean. She had plenty of sleep and good food but just seemed off. I have off days too, so I understand. But I cried over it still when she fell asleep.

I cried over the fact that she is growing so fast, and some nights, it hits me heavy, like right in the gut. Tonight, she fell asleep in my arms like she does most nights, but I stayed with her extra long so I could feel her full body weight and I sang these song lyrics quietly,

Lord, I need You, Oh, I need You.

Every hour I need You.

My one request, my righteousness.

Oh, God, how I need You.

Teach my heart to rise to You,

When temptation comes my way.

When I cannot stand, I'll fall on You.

Jesus, you're my hope and stay.

As I was singing, I remembered that my mom loves that song by Matt Redman. And if I were little, I'm sure she would sing it over me. Maybe I'm just tired or weary. But I'm on vacation, so I'm not sure how I could be weary other than my weaknesses and my flesh trying to rule.

On a funny note, Eden sent her first text message on my phone before bed, which she rarely ever gets to use. I noticed it after she fell asleep. She wrote:

12?(,;???;(??(bbbgbvccvxc.   Hbjnnjbhggdgv.   Cbb-nbbbbbbbbbbcxxx. Nvm

I imagine that's what the thoughts of my scrambled brain looks like at times. My emotions can be all over the place if I'm not careful to take my thoughts captive. I can spiral into a ditch of woes.

I think as I'm growing older in the Lord, and especially after having a child, I'm beginning to understand more and more the importance of the verse that says "take every thought captive and make it obedient to Christ." (2 Corinthians 10:5)

Of course, if we are not taking our thoughts captive then what we are thinking will slip out of our mouths. So in connections with our thoughts it is also critical that we keep a guard over our tongues (Psalm 141:3). The Pulpit Commentary on this verse says "keep the door of my lips. David's was a hasty, impetuous temper, which required sharp control." He strove to "keep his own mouth with a bridle" and to "be dumb with silence…"

Since we are on the topic of our minds running everywhere, I'm so grateful that our luggage was recovered so that I can stop thinking about it, but while it was lost, I learned that I could live on very little. Since the bag arrived, I have only used a few things from inside. It's amazing how much I packed and how little I need. I fear that I live that way too. It makes me think that maybe today is a good day to give something away or to go through that closet and give away a few pieces of clothing that hasn't been worn in a while or go through the children's clothes that are too small and bless someone else with them.

This past week I met with a dear friend for lunch out here in California, and she surprised me with a giant bag of hardly worn little girl clothes all for Eden that fit perfectly. The bag weighed more than Eden weighs! In just these few days I have already clothed Eden from that bag several times. It blessed my heart beyond measure.

It's late now, so goodnight to all my scrambled brain mom friends out there. May God give our hearts and minds rest tonight.

"And why are you worried about clothing? Observe how the lilies of the field grow; they do not toil nor do they spin."

Matthew 6:28

June 12, 2019

SURE, SOMETIMES I QUESTION MY PARENTING.
BUT TO BE HONEST, SOMETIMES I QUESTION MY CHILD'S CHILDING.

QUESTIONS

une 13, 2019

I'm glad our lost luggage was found because Eden's Children's Bible was in there, and tonight, we read a lot out of it. Eden asked if Elijah was a Christian, and if Baal was a Christian, and if the lady and her son with the oil story were Christians. Then she asked if she was a Christian.

We hadn't had a spiritual talk in a while where she asks me questions like this. In fact, we have had some hard days between our luggage being lost, and her battling constipation, so such a conversation was a true gift from God. I was glad to see when we arrived at our first vacation home that one of our spiritual conversations about not worshipping an idol had stuck in her head. The home had two Buddha-like icons that she turned the face around and said, "No good!" I like her thinking.

≈ GOODBYES ≈

"Therefore humble yourselves under the mighty hand of God, that He may exalt you at the proper time,"

≈1 Peter 5:6

*J*une 14, 2019

We took Eden to Disneyland for the first time last Tuesday. It was a great time. We went to Toontown, and I think Eden could have ridden on the carousel the entire day. She liked it so much that I took her three times. She rode a horse that went high up, and on the way down I would kiss her cheek. Emilio took pictures to capture every second. Then we went on a little train ride, the Dumbo ride, and to It's a Small World.

Speaking of it's a small world, we were just at the airport to go back to Texas when I spotted a couple that I gave tracts to yesterday. We were in Balboa at a hole-in-the-wall fish and chips restaurant. They said they were from Italy. I told them my family was from Piedmont, Italy and the man said that he travels there all the time. At that time, they were with their son, who looked to be in his forties, and a granddaughter. Now it was just the two of them, so I imagine they were heading back home all the way across the world.

The lady recognized me and gave me a big smile. Who knows what sort of pain her heart was in to have to leave her son behind. At that restaurant, I gave the whole family tracts. Maybe my face will be a reminder of the Gospel and God's faithfulness. What are the chances that I'd run into them? It is, indeed, a small world. I can only hope and pray I see all their faces in heaven where we will never have to say goodbye and we can all eat around the Master's table.

Speaking of saying goodbye, Eden got to meet Mickey and Minnie and Goofy. I'm sure she didn't want to say goodbye to them either. And the Disneyland band was playing in the streets with their incredible instrumental music. I could smell caramel popcorn in the air and hot dogs, and children were screaming for joy. I told Eden that Heaven would probably be similar in that we will be singing in the streets and eating delicious food with the Lord. And it will be absent of sin and trouble.

Then she and I started singing one of our tunes as the band played in the background:

> *When the saints go marching in*
> *When the saints go marching in!*
> *Oh, how I want to be in that number,*
> *When the saints go marching in!*

I have explained that not everyone will be marching into heaven, but the Christians will. And I want her to be in that number.

"Therefore humble yourselves under the mighty hand of God, that He may exalt you at the proper time,"

—1 Peter 5:6

⤳ NEAR ⤳

"This poor one cried out and the LORD heard, and from all his distress He saved him."

⤳Psalm 34:7

June 15, 2019

We left our pleasant stay in Corona Del Mar, California and headed for Newport to stay at our new location until Wednesday. The home in Newport has an incredible view of the Balboa Peninsula, and we can see boats all throughout the day, which is so calming to the soul.

At the beach, I met a lady and her three children while we were out playing in the sand. I found out she was a Mormon. I gave her a gospel tract, and she seemed grateful. She also seemed to express that she was really grieving the growing process of her children, and mentioned she had just weaned her last child from nursing and was struggling through it. So, I told her about my book *Struggles and Sunshine* and to look for it on Amazon.

The same day we received a text message that one of our dear church members had passed out at home and was taken to the hospital in an ambulance. It was the same member, JoAnn, who had helped us find our luggage at the airport. We began praying for her full recovery. A few hours later, we received a text that the nurses assigned to her care had really interesting names…Trish and Emilia.

At first, I thought it was a joke. My husband, Emilio, has been JoAnn's pastor for many years. It seemed impossible that the two people responsible for taking care of her had names so similar to ours. What kindness of the Lord to do that.

Tonight before bed, Eden said, "Mama, Minnie needs an x-ray because she broke her arm petting a cat named Emilio. It was a different cat than Simba. Can you tend to her Mama?" Then she added, "We need to set her arm...but she might cry with this."

Eden knows much about fixing broken arms because she broke hers in August of 2018. She was trying to pet a cat named Simba while standing on a landscaping rock and fell. I knew something was very wrong when she just laid in the grass and would not get up. It still pains me to write about it. She was only a few feet from me when I ran and picked her up, looked at her arm, and knew right away she was seriously hurt. I put her in our jogger, dropped my dog's leash, and started running as fast as I could, pushing her home. I sang one of Eden's favorite songs by Sovereign Grace Music called *Ready Set Go* as I ran to try to get her to stop crying.

When we got home (which was a couple of blocks away), I told Emilio we needed to go right away to the hospital. That night they confirmed her arm was broken. It was mortifying, to say the least. I was up throughout the night for days tending to her. Looking back on it now I can see the good that came from it because it was one of the most special times in terms of our closeness. I was Eden's great comfort in her pain, which ministered to me about how God is very near to His children when we are wounded. He pays special attention to those that are afflicted. Psalm 34:18 says, "The LORD is near to the brokenhearted, And saves those who are crushed in spirit." Another great kindness from Him.

"This poor one cried out and the LORD heard, and from all his distress He saved him."

Psalm 34:7

⤙ ANCHOR ⤚

"This hope we have as an anchor of the soul, a hope both sure and steadfast and one which enters within the veil,"

⟞Hebrews 6:19

*J*une 16, 2019

Eden played very sweetly tonight before bed. We are still at the vacation home, and she found a set of coasters with anchors on them. She gave one to Emilio as a gift, then me and then herself. It was so sweet. She seemed so proud to be able to present us with gifts. I can only hope and pray Hebrew 6:19 will be an anchor to her soul, and ours too.

One more thing. Maybe I should eat more junk food and go on vacation more because Eden said, "Your tummy looks soooo cute." It just warmed my heart.

"This hope we have as an anchor of the soul, a hope both sure and steadfast and one which enters within the veil,"

⟞Hebrews 6:19

⪼ SMALL ⪻

June 17, 2019

I had a terrific day on our vacation with Eden, until after her nap, when I couldn't console her. She just seemed to wake up fussy. Her nap had been short. Maybe she needed to sleep longer. Or perhaps she needed more milk. I knew she was suffering some constipation, so maybe that was it. I couldn't figure it out, and she was just crazy with it all.

So, I took her out of the house on a one-minute walk to the sand, and she stopped crying instantly. She was over everything as if nothing happened. I was not over everything that quick, though. Perhaps my pride was hurt because I didn't know how to fix her or understand what was wrong. I prayed with her about it all and called my mom, which helped a lot. Then Emilio pulled up and asked how things were going.

I said, "Well...why don't you tell him?" and she said, "I wanted a jellybean!"

I had forgotten that I had offered her a jellybean for trying to go potty, but one was not enough, she had wanted TWO. Maybe that was the reason for all her fussing. Only God knows at this point.

Then I got a message that my dear friend, Ray Comfort, was in the hospital again after being in and out for a week because of a terrible kidney stone. Hearing of his pain made mine with Eden a lot less severe. Lord, forgive us (me) for being moved so quickly by small things, and by small people! Help Ray's small stone, which is causing him big pain, to pass immediately so that he can save himself some pain. Amen. For any of you that know Ray, he wrote a booklet called *Save Yourself Some Pain*. It's great to hand out to people and to read for yourself. You can find it at LivingWaters.com.

I'm on the plane headed back to Texas writing all of this. It's about a three-hour flight and Eden has been sleeping the whole time. Emilio just tapped me to say we only have about "30 minutes left". I'm shocked. That was the fastest flight I've been on in a long time.

By the way, I failed to mention we took Eden on the Pirates of the Caribbean ride at Disneyland. I don't know what we were thinking, other than it had been 10 years or longer since we had ridden it that we had forgotten how terrible it was. There we skeletons everywhere, and darkness. Eden covered her ears, and I covered her eyes.

She told me, "The Pirates ride looked like it was going to the pit." Then she added, "The pit will be dark!" What truth. Immediately after the ride, she began singing a Christian song. Sometimes it takes us seeing darkness to understand how good being in the light truly is.

Speaking of darkness and light, Eden just woke up and looked out the window of the airplane at the sun setting above the dark clouds. It was a glorious pinkish/orange sunset like over the ocean. She pointed and said, "This is what it will look like when Jesus comes back."

"For the LORD God is a sun and shield; The LORD gives grace and glory; No good thing does He withhold from those who walk uprightly."

Psalm 84:11

DELIGHT

"Every good thing given and every perfect gift is from above, coming down from the Father of lights, with whom there is no variation or shifting shadow."

⎯James 1:17

June 18, 2019

Eden's arms have gotten so long that she now wraps her arms entirely around my neck. This week is the first I've felt her do this. I guess that's one positive to her growing. She can hug me more thoroughly. At one point, she grabbed my neck and pulled my face close to hers and kept us cheek to cheek. It was beyond special.

Tonight, before bed, I was admiring how adorable her arms looked as she was squatting to play with Play-Doh. I wanted to cry at how precious her hands looked. I sat down to play with the Play-Doh too when she stood up, leaned against the wall, and said, "Is this my Mama?!" And came and hugged me. It was as if she was admiring me playing with her Play-Doh. It all made me think of the Lord, and how He loves to watch over us and delight in us delighting in His things.

"Every good thing given and every perfect gift is from above, coming down from the Father of lights, with whom there is no variation or shifting shadow."

⎯James 1:17

⤜ ASSEMBLE ⤛

"…and let us consider how to stimulate one another to love and good deeds, not forsaking our own assembling together, as is the habit of some, but encouraging one another; and all the more as you see the day drawing near."

⇒Hebrews 10:24-25

*J*une 19, 2019

Tonight, Eden said while playing in her bedroom, "I like going to church."

"Why?" I asked.

She said, "Well…it's good for the heart."

And, indeed, that is true.

"…and let us consider how to stimulate one another to love and good deeds, not forsaking our own assembling together, as is the habit of some, but encouraging one another; and all the more as you see the day drawing near."

⇒Hebrews 10:24-25

∞ TRANSFORM ∞

"Remember those who led you, who spoke the word of God to you; and considering the result of their conduct, imitate their faith."

═Hebrews 13:7

*J*une 21, 2019

I got my Realtors License earlier this year, and yesterday, I showed three properties to my first clients. They are a Christian family that wants to relocate from Colorado to Texas and go to our church, which is a huge blessing. I prayed yesterday that the showings would be fruitful and that they would find the best house for them to enjoy as a family. What was extra special was that I was able to bring Eden and Emilio along with me, and they were there when the family decided upon the first home I showed them, a two-story new build. Eden loved the stairs in that home. The entire time we were there, she only wanted to go up and down the stairs. It's funny how much fun that is as a kid, but as an adult we can become out of breath fast.

Upon leaving, I told the sales rep about my first book, *Struggles and Sunshine*, and about all six of Ray Comfort's gospel films that are free to watch online. I'm praying the sale of this home will go through, and that Eden and I will be able to play on those stairs one day soon.

"Lord, Your Word says in Ecclesiastes 3:10 'Whatever your hand finds, do it with all your might.' I pray for my sisters reading this that you would bless the work of our hands. That we would sense you carrying us through good days, hard days, prosperous days, lean days, all days. Amen"

Before bed, I turned on Eden's Hello Kitty radio to some worship music. It's an old fashion radio that plays cassette tapes and CDs and has an antenna (some of you may still have one and laugh that I said it was "old fashion"). Eden's grandpa, who we call Ompiee, put it on The Way radio station a few nights ago. I'm typically not into contemporary Christian music because it tends to be theologically weak, but tonight I had it on while Eden was putting butterfly stickers up on her wall.

As she was sticking one of her butterflies on, I said, "That's what God does with the Christian Eden. He changes us from a caterpillar to a butterfly, and lets us soar and fly." Then I prayed in my heart that she would be a butterfly (Christian) one day soon. The combination of watching her little hands delight in putting the stickers on the wall, and hearing the worship music that reminded me of when I first got saved, made me cry. Eden noticed my tears, so I assured her that I was worshiping God and was happy. She crawled in my lap while I cried, and seemed to enjoy it.

Then one of my tears dropped in her eye, which I thought would make her cry, but she started laughing, and so did I. It was a sweet time of worship and laughter. She seemed to come alive around the music, so I just continued to listen. Surprisingly, the songs ministered to me, and I had flashbacks of how God has brought me out of darkness and into His marvelous light. Let's not be afraid to turn up the hymns and our favorite worship songs so that our children see us enjoy God, even if it produces tears of joy.

There are many worship songs that have ministered to Eden and me, which I've listed in the back of this book. For an even fuller list, grab a copy of my first book *Struggles and Sunshine*. Many of these songs we have played over and over nightly as my mom (who Eden calls Meesie) comes over and plays with us. I have her over almost every night even if it is just for an hour. Many times it is longer and it is special and has become part of our nighttime bedtime routine. Meesie loves the worship too and will dance and run around (skip) in the bedroom and Eden goes crazy.

"Remember those who led you, who spoke the word of God to you; and considering the result of their conduct, imitate their faith."

Hebrews 13:7

"Your word is a lamp to my feet And a light to my path."

⊸Psalm 119:105

June 27, 2019

I decided my guest bathroom needed new soap. You know the foam kind you never use for yourself (at least I typically don't), but want others to enjoy while washing their hands? That's the kind I wanted, so I decided to take a quick trip to the Bath and Body Works store.

A lady employee welcomed Eden and I as soon as we walked in and then kept staring at Eden. She finally came over and said, "I used to do my daughters' hair just like that!" Then she added, "I feel so old. My one daughter is a teen, and the other is getting married any day now, so it's just all over for me."

It was hard to hear her say those words. They seemed to haunt her. Right then, I got out my phone and pulled up my book *Struggles and Sunshine* and told her perhaps it would be a good read for her since it deals a lot with grief in terms of our children growing up. She took a picture of it, and it seemed promising that she would get a copy. I pray she does, as I believe it will minister to her based on the encouraging feedback I have received from other ladies that have read it.

One such dear lady named Karen wrote to me saying, "So many words touched my soul." She sent me several messages as she was reading through the book. I thought they are worth recording here.

"Your book is making me cry. I relate so much. It's so encouraging; you are such a special blessed mommy!!! My only problem, I wish I would have had this book when Riggs (her son) was born!!!

Riggs said, please read one more (entry). We read like five and Harwell (her husband) came and joined in the last one. You are for encouraging this family so much, and I pray so many will get this book!!!

Glory to God in the Highest!!! God bless the Ramos family richly, more and more. I hope you can do a Part 2 book. Thank you for opening up your heart to moms, may it go far and wide!!!

The book is so well done, Glory to God. I have never heard of this idea of confessions from a Mother. It's such a blessed thing because I think so many women go through these thoughts, but to have this pointing to Jesus and to see they are not alone. This will make such good baby shower gifts! Etc...."

She wrote to me again, *"We couldn't put your book down tonight. Riggs kept saying 'one more.' I've been reading it over an hour. We cried and laughed. It fills us with joy. How could I possibly write a review of how much I love this book? I'll have to pray for God to give me the words. You've shared Eden Joy with this book in such a powerful way to give God much Glory. This book, for sure, can teach women to love their children in a bigger, more Christ-like way. Such a joyful way to go to bed sharing in the struggles and joys of motherhood. Eden Joy's name is perfect!!! She is so blessed and blesses you all, and us that have this privilege to share in your motherhood. Lord, may you give us generations from these dear children that worship You forever and ever. Eden Joy is stamped on our heart!"*

And one last message: *"Reading Job, the part where God is talking to him, and your book, caused my aching heart to turn to joy tonight. Thank you for being obedient to stir up the mother's to love and good works."*

She even wrote saying her *"13-year-old old son stayed up till 2:00am reading Struggles and Sunshine and slept with a copy."* It is stories like these that will keep me writing.

It reminds me of the proverb that says, "Like cold water to a weary soul, So is good news from a distant land." (Proverbs 25:25)

A missionary friend in Mexico named Cassi said this: "I just love how you always tie a situation or a simple detail with the Word of God or a way that we can apply it to our lives. It is so encouraging and helpful for my journey as a mom as well. Everything I read has touched my heart dearly, especially the prayer section page 22 and the "come on" page 34."

A sister at church named Terri said, "Oh Trisha...you have no idea the sort of emotions you have stirred in me...I need to grab a box of Kleenex and cry for an hour somewhere alone. It's so good."

Another sister with the same name, but spelled differently (Tere) stayed up till 4:00am reading half the book. Then woke up the next day with thoughts of finishing it, and that night did just that.

What a blessing to touch people through written words. God was the first one to think of touching us with The Written Word (His Bible). I pray this book will touch Eden for now and eternity as well. Lord, save our children. Save the children of my readers. Comfort their hearts through written words, especially Your written word. Thank you that you are rich in love thank you that you are full of mercy (Ephesians 2:4) and you don't forget about your children in each generation (Psalm 119:90). Amen.

"Your word is a lamp to my feet And a light to my path."

Psalm 119:105

⤳ TEACH ⤳

*"Teach me your way oh Lord and I will walk in your truth,
give me an undivided heart that I may fear your name."*

⤳Psalm 86

June 28, 2019

Out of the blue today, I started, "Ma T's School of Manners, Biblical Studies, and Education." I pretended to be a teacher named Ma T, which wasn't difficult because it is short for Mama Trish, and also because I was once a teacher. Years ago, I went to school to be an educator, teaching in Southern California for several grade levels all the way from Kindergarten to grade 12. But, my heart just wasn't into teaching about the ABC's and 123's. Instead, my heart's desire was to evangelize and teach people the ways of God. Today though, was about teaching all of those things to Eden and the rest of the "class." And God had changed my heart to be fully into it and thoroughly enjoying it.

I would never have dreamed that I would one day educate my child. What a blessing! And Eden couldn't get enough of Ma T's teaching. We pretended every stuffed animal of hers was a student. And oh, how I wish I could turn all her animals into children of mine. If I had it all to do over again I would have as many children as I could. We had much fun. Eden laughed. I laughed. She especially loved when my pointer pointed to the numbers and letters on the big books I had propped up. Her animals even took turns guessing the names of the numbers. I think Eden learned how to count from 1-30 today, or pretty close to it. We handed out rewards to every animal that participated. Naturally, Eden was chosen as my helper.

Of course, our model for teaching comes from God. He has been instructing since the beginning of time. He instructed Adam, and his chosen helper, Eve, to "be fruitful and multiply, and fill the earth, and subdue it; and rule over the fish of the sea and over the birds of the sky and over every living thing that moves on the earth." (Genesis 1:22) Let's always look to Him on how to rightly instruct our children.

And on the days when our little one's disobedience makes teaching especially challenging, know that God understands. He had the first disobedient "students" if you will. And they were full-grown (hint: Adam and Eve).

A few verses to enjoy and meditate on:

Kings 8:36

May You hear from heaven and forgive the sin of Your servants, Your people Israel, so that You may teach them the good way in which they should walk. May You send rain on the land that You gave Your people as an inheritance.

Psalm 25:4

Show me Your ways, O LORD; teach me Your paths.

Psalm 25:5

Guide me in Your truth and teach me, for You are the God of my salvation; all day long I wait for You.

Psalm 27:11

Teach me Your way, O LORD, and lead me on a level path, because of my oppressors.

Psalm 119:68

You are good and do good; teach me Your statutes.

Lord, any mom, whether a homeschool mom or not, knows she wants her children to succeed in school. Help us as Your students to sit and listen and learn Your ways and excel in Your school so that we can in turn train them in an honorable and upright way. Amen.

"Teach me your way oh Lord and I will walk in your truth, give me an undivided heart that I may fear your name."

—Psalm 86

"Whenever the rainbow appears in the clouds, I will see it and remember the everlasting covenant between God and all living creatures of every kind on the earth."

⇒Genesis 9:16

*J*uly 5, 2019

Eden and I did last night's family devotion, just the two of us. Emilio was deep in study and we didn't want to disturb his concentration. Somehow we started singing "Away in a Manger." Even though it's summer, we were reading about the birth of Jesus, so it felt very much like Christmas. We began talking about the frankincense that was given as a gift to Jesus. I even went into my pantry and pulled up frankincense oil so Eden could smell it. I began putting some on her feet, and I told her about the lady in the Bible that put some on Jesus' feet.

I asked her, "Do you remember what she did with her hair?"

Eden answered by bending over a bit and rubbing her own feet, indicating that the woman washed His feet. Then she said, "Judas didn't like it." How right she was.

Last year I had taught Eden that Judas was watching the woman wash Jesus' feet with the expensive oil, and said, "What a waste!" He felt that they could sell the oil for a high price and give the money to the poor, but, secretly, he just wanted it for himself.

We went back to the sofa and closed our devotional time by singing "Away in a Manger" and praying for a bit.

The Bible is the most excellent tool for teaching children. God made His book deeply captivating for young minds and old minds alike. He doesn't leave out any detail and includes the good, the bad, and the ugly. Children are especially drawn to know what the "bad people" are doing. In her children's bible someone is always in some sort of bind or in sin or has an issue with their health and so Eden is always intrigued to find out how it will be resolved. And if you've ever heard that B.I.B.L.E stands for:

B: Basic

I: Instructions

B: Before

L: Leaving

E: Earth

It's true. The bible is "basic instructions before leaving earth."

May we (I) not undermine the power of the written Word to teach and instruct and exhort and correct our children. In fact, I see no age limit when I read Hebrews 4:12:

"For the word of God is living and active and sharper than any two-edged sword, and piercing as far as the division of soul and spirit, of both joints and marrow, and able to judge the thoughts and intentions of the heart."

Later in the day, I was responding to an email from a brother named Mark (one of the assistants to Ken Ham, the builder of Noah's Ark in Kentucky). I'm hoping he will give the green light to them carrying Struggles and Sunshine in their bookstore, which would be a huge blessing. As I was typing, I noticed the sky outside looked very orange. When I stepped outside, I saw a giant, full-sized rainbow. "Maybe it's a sign they will carry my book," I laughed to myself.

What a tremendous ministry Ken Ham has in Answers in Genesis. If any of my readers have not been to the Ark

Encounter, I pray you will get to see it during your lifetime. I was there opening day, and it was an incredible and impactful reminder of God's promise to His people.

"Whenever the rainbow appears in the clouds, I will see it and remember the everlasting covenant between God and all living creatures of every kind on the earth."

⟨Genesis 9:16

⋙ WATCHING ⋘

"If I should count them, they would outnumber the sand.
When I awake, I am still with You."

Psalm 139:18

*J*uly 6, 2019

I finally went to the doctor today after experiencing signs of sickness. I wanted to make sure I didn't have strep throat (I didn't). The doctor prescribed an antibiotic since I've been getting sick like clockwork about every two months. I can't remember the last time I took an antibiotic. It could be as far back as six years ago when I went to Mexico and got food poisoning. Before that, it could be as far back as my childhood. I was one of those children that never missed school. I didn't want to miss out on anything, so I had to be on my last leg to stay home from school.

The same is true of me for church. Unless I have a contagious sickness, I am there. When on our yearly vacation to California, we look forward to visiting a church pastored by our friend Philip DeCourcy. This year we didn't make it though. Every time we planned to go, something came up, such as Eden battling constipation.

One such Sunday was Father's Day. We had fully planned to go to church but just couldn't make it out the door on time. So, after watching our service back home via the Internet, Eden and I went for a walk on the Balboa Peninsula while Emilio watched a ball game. We walked where the Fun Zone is located, and after buying a little ice cream, passing out a few tracts, and enjoying the day, we ran into, of all people, Pastor Philip DeCourcy and his whole family. I was shocked, to say the least. It was so kind of God to bring us together like that. We got on the topic of children, naturally, as I was holding Eden, and they asked if we wanted more. I said, "Oh yes, but we are old and Emilio feels very old."

Pastor Phillip said, "Tell Emilio that 40 is the new 30 and 50 is the new 40!"

Then his wife said, "Maybe that is why we ran into you."

I'm glad the Lord directed my steps in such a special way. (Proverbs 16:9)

Eden is sleeping as I write. She went down early tonight because I have been giving her a lot of exercise. We ate dinner at Hat Creek Burger Co., where they have an incredible area for kids to play. And boy did we play. Eden ran so much that she was practically ready to go to bed when we got home. I miss her when she sleeps, though. I miss seeing the funny things she does. I miss her saying "I love you Mama," and I miss her learning new things.

So, I watch over her a lot while she sleeps. Many nights I write for an hour or two or even three while sitting beside her in bed. That's a lot of watching, but it doesn't compare to how much God watches over us. Psalm 121:4 says, "Behold, He who keeps Israel will neither slumber nor sleep."

What a comforting thought. My longing to watch over Eden while she sleeps was designed by our great God, who does the very same thing for us! Rest tonight, dear one, in the fact that He knows all things, isn't surprised by anything and can work out very difficult things for your and my good (Romans 8:28).

Lord, I pray for my sisters who are battling sadness and maybe just don't know why. Or for those that are battling the reality of their children growing or being grown and already moved out and the pain all of that can bring upon the heart of a mom. Lord, You know we are in this fallen world. You are kind when you said on so many occasions to your people, "Do not fear." You know just how fearful and worried and troubled little creatures we can be. Thank you Lord that when the disciples feared for You to leave them when You had to go to the cross, you promised a Comforter. Thank you for the Holy Spirit. Thank you for the comfort He brings to our hearts. We need it, Lord and You know it. Thank you that you know all things. Thank you that You will be with us when we wake.

"If I should count them, they would outnumber the sand. When I awake, I am still with You."

Psalm 139:18

Eden running at Hat Creek Burger Co.

Eden being silly doing her "Meesie" face.
My mom (Meesie) used to make this same face when she was a child.

⋙ ETERNAL ⋘

"And we know that the Son of God is come, and hath given us an understanding, that we may know him that is true, and we are in him that is true, even in his Son Jesus Christ. This is the true God, and eternal life."

⋍1 John 5:20

July 7, 2019

Tonight, I was watching a film Emilio is in called *American Gospel*. One of the people interviewed for the movie recounted how every time he got a new car, the newness would wear off. So he would get another car, only to have the newness wear off again, and on and on. But when he met Jesus, he realized Christ would never end and since He is eternal and gives us a never-ending newness of life to walk in (Romans 6:4) he had a joy that was lasting.

This man's story made me think of the many toys and animals and dolls that Eden has that occupy both her bedroom and her school/playroom. She's always excited to get new things, but their luster doesn't last. Lord, help Eden to see what the person in *American Gospel* saw. I know she is into all her toys and the "next thing," but show her that Jesus will not have an end like a good film does or playtime does or when we have to say goodbye. He will always be. He lives on.

Think of the person that has given you a lot of gifts. That person is more of a gift than any gift they could ever give you (or at least they should be), which reminds me of the Lord. He has given me (and you) a lot of gifts, but nothing compares to the gift of Himself on the cross.

Before bed, I read this:

Only One Life - By C.T. Studd

Two little lines I heard one day,
Traveling along life's busy way;
Bringing conviction to my heart,
And from my mind would not depart;
Only one life, 'twill soon be past,
Only what's done for Christ will last.

Only one life, yes only one,
Soon will its fleeting hours be done;
Then, in 'that day' my Lord to meet,
And stand before His Judgment seat;
Only one life, 'twill soon be past,
Only what's done for Christ will last.

Only one life, the still small voice,
Gently pleads for a better choice;
Bidding me selfish aims to leave,
And to God's holy will to cleave;
Only one life, 'twill soon be past,
Only what's done for Christ will last.

Only one life, a few brief years,
Each with its burdens, hopes, and fears;
Each with its clays I must fulfill,
living for self or in His will;
Only one life, 'twill soon be past,
Only what's done for Christ will last.

When this bright world would tempt me sore,
When Satan would a victory score;
When self would seek to have its way,
Then help me Lord with joy to say;
Only one life, 'twill soon be past,
Only what's done for Christ will last.

Give me Father, a purpose deep,
In joy or sorrow Thy word to keep;
Faithful and true what e'er the strife,
Pleasing Thee in my daily life;
Only one life, 'twill soon be past,
Only what's done for Christ will last.

Oh let my love with fervor burn,
And from the world now let me turn;
Living for Thee, and Thee alone,
Bringing Thee pleasure on Thy throne;
Only one life, 'twill soon be past,
Only what's done for Christ will last.

Only one life, yes only one,
Now let me say,"Thy will be done";
And when at last I'll hear the call,
I know I'll say "twas worth it all";
Only one life,'twill soon be past,
Only what's done for Christ will last.

"And we know that the Son of God is come, and hath given us an understanding, that we may know him that is true, and we are in him that is true, even in his Son Jesus Christ. This is the true God, and eternal life."

1 John 5:20

⟨ REST ⟩

"O clap your hands, all peoples;
Shout to God with the voice of joy."

⟨Psalm 47:1

July 9, 2019

I've been reading to Eden from *The Beginners Bible* every night before bed. We have recently purposed to go through every page. As I was reading, we came to the part where Pharaoh's army is chasing after the Israelites. The army is right on the heels of the Israelites, ready to attack when God confuses them with a cloud so that they could not see in front of them, and Moses is ultimately able to lead the people out of Egypt.

I was sure Eden was no longer paying any attention at this point, but she suddenly started clapping and clapping for their success. May I learn to rejoice over God's Word like that! May all of us reading this do the same.

Speaking of learning to rejoice, I'm sure Eden grew last night, which made me want to cry a river. I had to purpose to master my feelings and not allow them to dominate me. I'm sure she grew because she slept 13 hours last night, and then napped for two more. I held her a lot during her nap and was comforted that she was still small in my arms, but then this evening, I started to notice that her forearms were not as chubby. I'm happy she is growing, don't get me wrong, but if I overthink about how quickly time has passed, I will go into an hour-long cry fest. It didn't help that she tried to put her pants on. I laughed though because she had her two legs in one pant leg.

All of this got me to thinking about endless crying, and how many times I have done convalescent ministry where people are bound to bed because of old age and things of that nature. One particular lady was laying on her side alone in her room, crying. When we asked her what was wrong, she just kept crying. It breaks my heart now thinking about it even more than it did then. But then I remembered another lady named Naomi that was around 95 years old and every time we would go in her room there was a brightness about it. She had a lot of well-kept things and knew the Bible better than any of us young people did. What struck me is that she was probably older than the other lady, could hardly see, her back was rounded when she sat up, and could barely walk, but all she wanted was someone to read the Bible to her. She would close her eyes to listen.

One brother went back Sunday after Sunday to do this for her. She told us that she is always amazed that she is alive when she wakes up each morning, and that "God must not be done with her." She had no family to visit her. Her children were nowhere to be found, and her husband was gone, but the Lord was not. She had light in her eyes even though her eyesight had grown dim. And it was contagious. Lord help us to rest in your grace day-to-day. Amen.

"O clap your hands, all peoples;
Shout to God with the voice of joy."

Psalm 47:1

uly 10, 2019

YOU ARE THE MOTHER THAT GOD ASSIGNED TO YOUR
CHILDREN. THIS TRUTH SHOULD STIR YOU TO PUT
YOUR WHOLE HEART AND SOUL INTO LOVING YOUR
CHILDREN, AND IT SHOULD FILL YOUR HEART WITH
PEACE, KNOWING THAT GOD NEVER MAKES MISTAKES.

⤍ RUN ⤏

*"Then you will look and be radiant, and your heart will tremble
and rejoice, because the riches of the sea will be brought to you,
and the wealth of the nations will come to you."*

⟜Isaiah 60:5

*J*uly 11, 2019

It's hard for me to move when Eden is napping like she is right now. I don't mean that I want to be quiet and not make a peep to wake her (though that is true). And I don't mean it's hard to move because she is trapping me by lying on my legs though that is true too. What I mean is, I don't want to ever move from this place in time. I want to stay right here in this moment.

I'm sure all of these feelings are because I'm older, and she is my only child. And I feel like I missed out on so much joy the first half of my life because of foolish unbiblical and ungodly views of children. In my first book, *Struggles and Sunshine*, I go into this in more detail.

I was thinking of some things I would like to do over if I could have ten years of my life back. I guess the thought crossed my mind because we gathered as a family on the 4th of July to fellowship and play games. One game was for every person to answer different questions that I had thought of and written out. No one knew the questions, but me. Even Eden got some such as, "What is your favorite worship song?" She answered, "Rejoice, Rejoice Oh Daughter of Zion." And "What would you rather be? An eagle or a cheetah?" To which she answered, "A cheetah!" And the family roared in laughter.

One question that turned out to be a favorite was, "Would you rather have 10 million dollars or be ten years younger?" I chose to be ten years younger because then I could have more kids (God willing) and sin less (hopefully) by loving my mom more and serving the church more. Which are all things I do now, but time is just so precious, much more valuable to me than money and those things are very valuable to me.

Speaking of time, a sister from our bible study was pouring out her heart about how hard it is that her son is turning 5. He now wants to put on his seatbelt and get out of the car with no help. I could relate so much as late last night I was hit with an aching heart about how much Eden has grown, but was comforted that "my times are in His hands" (Psalm 31:15). And that I need to do as Colossians 3 says and "fix my eyes on things above and not on earthly things." I must admit this is hard to do, and it can feel like a war at times. But we fight as God is fighting with us as we work out our salvation with fear and trembling (Philippians 2:12).

The sister said we must focus on ministry today. Not past ministry or future ministry, but what is in front of us now.

What ministry is in front of you today? Is it socks on the floor or a bed to make or dishes to clean or bills to pay or something to clean out (like a drawer that is bursting at the seams) or a person to send a thank you note to or your mom to call (or someone else's mom to encourage them). We are not alone in the race of grief and losses and suffering. Like Elisabeth Elliot says, "We must go through many little deaths before we die." Let's choose today to set our minds on things above, and let God's grace carry us and do the next thing in front of you.

Lord, touch my sisters' as they read this book. Focus our hearts not to grumble and complain, but rather to give thanks because that is Your will. (1 Thessalonians 5:17) And grant us the strength to press on and press into You. Amen. Now let me get up, while Eden naps, and clean my room that looks like a Texas tornado hit it.

After naptime, I was talking to Eden about Psalm 119 and the verse that says, "I will run the way of your commandments for You will enlarge my heart." I asked if she remembers people running down the street randomly, and how she always asks me, "What are they doing, Mama?"

It must look funny to a child to see people running for no apparent reason. She probably is thinking, "Who is chasing them?" or "Is something wrong?" But I always tell her that they are doing it for their health, "Like how Papa goes to the gym." They are exercising with the purpose to build endurance and strength, and perhaps to live longer. She seemed to remember all this, so I explained that runners tend to have enlarged hearts. (Now that I think about it, it's remarkable that the writer of Psalm 119 touches on this bit of medical knowledge if you will. Perhaps he was more advanced in his thinking than we realize).

Then I told Eden if she "runs the way of God's commandments, that God will make her spiritual heart big." Oh, how we need the stamina to do this. And what a reward and promise God's Word gives to us when we run on his narrow path. Does your heart feel weak, dear sister? Does your heart ache from losses or changes or difficulties in this life? Run in His way, run after His commandments, and He will tend to your heart.

Before bed tonight, Eden did something wonderful. She was very quiet, and I looked over to see her doing something on a giant calculator. She came over to me and said, "Look, Mama, I pulled up the (Unpopular) movie on my "phone."

I said, "Wow."

She said, "Absolutely."

That's a new word for her, and she used it correctly. Next, I want her to understand the Gospel correctly. That is a comforting thing about her getting older. Absolutely!

> *"Then you will look and be radiant, and your heart will tremble and rejoice, because the riches of the sea will be brought to you, and the wealth of the nations will come to you."*
>
> Isaiah 60:5

Eden holding her giant calculator "phone" and an UnpopularTheMovie.com card.

⟨⟨ INSTRUMENT ⟩⟩

"For I am convinced that neither death, nor life, nor angels,
nor principalities, nor things present, nor things to come, nor
powers, nor height, nor depth, nor any other created thing, will
be able to separate us from the love of God, which is in Christ
Jesus our Lord."

⟨Romans 8:38-39

*J*uly 13, 2019

It's hard to think that two weeks have already passed, but this picture was taken after church on June 30. I took out my guitar and started singing an old song from when I first got saved from David Ruis,

> *"It's our confession Lord that we are weak,*
> *So very weak but You are strong,*
> *And though we've nothing Lord to lay at Your feet*
> *We come to Your feet and say help us along."*

As I was singing, Eden grabbed her toy dog and started swaying with it to the music, singing along with me with heartfelt emotion in her face. This is the first time she's shown such expression during worship. It was notable in my mind, and Emilio even stopped to snap a picture (which he is not into taking pictures often).

We continued singing,

> *"A broken heart and a contrite spirit, You have yet to deny.*
> *Your heart of mercy beats with loves strong current,*
> *Let the river flow by Your Spirit now Lord we cry.*

Let your mercies fall from heaven sweet mercies flow from heaven,

New mercies for today, shower them down Lord as we pray."

May God give Eden a voice and a heart to worship the King humbly, in Spirit and in Truth. May it be true of all of my dear reader's children as well. May God cause our children to delight in worship and to sing of His praises all their lives. Which reminds me of a verse I have been meditating on lately in Eph 5:19 that says, "Sing and make music in your heart to the Lord." What struck me about this one sentence verse is that it *doesn't* say "worry with your heart", or "let your heart be troubled", or "let your heart be idle" or "let your heart be in stagnant". But rather we are to *make* music in our heart. We are to do something of course. We are to be busy about something and it's making music. Isn't it amazing that our heart can be an instrument? Think of it like a guitar or like a violin or piano. It might be out of tune and need some fine tuning but the more we practice singing hymns and spiritual songs and scripture the more in tune our hearts will become. Sort of like exercise. The more you do it the more your body craves it. Or the more sweets you eat the more you crave them. The same is true with scripture. The more scripture you hide in your heart (Psalm 119:11) the more you will crave to continue in it,

And in the words of Fernando Ortega's song (taken from the Psalms), he sings,

"I will sing to the Lord all my life I will sing praises to my God. As long I live...praises to the Lord oh my soul. Singing glory, glory, glory to the Lamb. All praises and honor forever and ever Amen."

"For I am convinced that neither death, nor life, nor angels, nor principalities, nor things present, nor things to come, nor powers, nor height, nor depth, nor any other created thing, will be able to separate us from the love of God, which is in Christ Jesus our Lord."

Romans 8:38-39

Eden holding her toy dog.

❧ SERVING ☙

"Whatever you do, whether you eat or drink…do all to the glory of God."

≡1 Corinthians 10:31

July 14, 2019

We ate at Chick-Fil-A today. It was nice to see Eden sitting so sweetly at the table. And I enjoyed serving her. My mom met us there, and I had food ready for her. There was something so peaceful about it and precious. It was fun too as if I had two kids. I even gave my mom her own kiddie placemat. She didn't mind one bit. Then we went into the play area and met a little girl named "Liberty," which is a cute name and very patriotic and reminded me of one of the Christian "Freedom Kids" videos we watch on YouTube. One of the little girls that dance to scripture songs is named "Liberty." I handed her mom an Unpopular gospel tract to which she said, "Oh yes! I have seen this and heard of it, but have not watched it yet, so thank you!"

Eden seemed to delight in the ice cream, which she gladly turned in the toy that came with her Kid's Meal to get. I love wiping her face and cleaning her mess. I bet the Lord is looking forward to the day when He serves us at the Marriage Supper of the Lamb. And I'm sure He will delight in watching all his people eat each bite. It will bring Him so much joy I'm sure. The thought of Him serving us is just too much. Shouldn't it be us serving Him? But remember He had to wash the apostles' feet.

In the same way, He will feed us. He served them by washing their feet, and in heaven, He will serve us at a table. And I have a feeling our feet will no longer need washing.

"Whatever you do, whether you eat or drink…do all to the glory of God."

=1 Corinthians 10:31

⤴ ENTANGLEMENTS ⤴

*"And let us run with perseverance the race marked out for us,
fixing our eyes on Jesus, the pioneer and perfecter of faith."*

⇒Hebrews 12:1b

*J*uly 15, 2019

Yesterday at church, a dear brother was sharing how, after his son became sick with an illness, he realized he was watching too much television. The TV can sure be a time-waster. What an encouragement to see the Lord working to clear away the dross in this brother's life, and to know He is doing the same for us.

Let's evaluate today if there are any areas in our lives where we need to do some house cleaning if you would. Maybe it's not TV, but your phone or endless hours on Facebook scrolling through the pages of people who are not even in your life. I can certainly get caught up in those if I'm not careful. 2 Timothy 2:4 is an excellent verse to meditate on, "Don't be entangled in civilian affairs so that we can please our commanding officer."

Speaking of commanding, I let Emilio take command of the car today and chauffeur Eden and I around. She slept and looked so cozy with the beams of sunlight shining in the window. I had her covered with a scarf to keep her warm from the cold A/C and to hide her face from the sun. We drove past Chick-fil-A, and in my heart, I said, "I will never look at that restaurant the same again. I have never had a bad experience there, and now with Eden, it has only been fun, fun, fun."

The same goes for Sweet Frog yogurt store, the Dollar Tree, Sprouts and the pet store. We have our routines. It all reminds me of how her birth marked a new beginning of new things, just like the day of our spiritual birth. When we get saved, we have new eyes, much like you do after having a child. You see the world differently. Very differently. Sin becomes much more sinful, for example. Evil becomes unbearable to hear or see. And wickedness (like abortion and other mistreating of babies and children) is maddening.

Similarly, when we get saved, we see everything through a biblical lens. As if we are wearing special glasses that the world and unbelievers do not have on. We desire for them to see, to really see, but they're unable until they have the gift of salvation.

Father, grant Eden, and the children of all those reading this, special glasses necessary for seeing the world rightly. Glasses to see how transient everything in this world is and how vital eternal matters are. May they all come to a saving knowledge that comes through repentance and faith as they put their trust in the Lord Jesus. Amen

"And let us run with perseverance the race marked out for us, fixing our eyes on Jesus, the pioneer and perfecter of faith."

Hebrews 12:1b

⤛ TRIUMPH ⤜

"And we know that God causes all things to work together for good to those who love God, to those who are called according to His purpose."

⥊Romans 8:28

*J*uly 16, 2019

I believe that most parents are tempted to worship their child. We love ourselves so much that, naturally, since the child is part of us it comes easy to want to give our lives for them and do everything we can to meet their needs. These things are good, but the temptation to place our children first, above everyone, including the Lord, can be a real one.

As I was reading Eden her Children's Bible tonight, the thought crossed my mind that Mary (Jesus' mother) was highly blessed because she could worship her child and not commit idolatry. She could sing His praises (quite literally) day and night, and it be entirely right. To think of her singing something like "I love You Jesus, and You are the best. There's no one greater than You" would be sung with no error. Some might consider her blessed, too, because she didn't have to give her son up in marriage.

However, she had a much larger problem. He was going to be given up to a Bride that had spots and blemishes of the worst sort. A Bride that needed cleansing, an imperfect Bride; one that was in darkness, and would turn to their own way (Isaiah 53:6) as He suffered on the cross. Such an imperfect bride would be any mom's nightmare.

But God brought beauty out of it all. The cross and suffering was not the end. Salvation and resurrection would triumph at its maximum. It would triumph over all the letting go; over all the sin and pain. Jesus secured the Bride's salvation, which included his earthly mom, Mary! This truth should comfort moms of sons on a practical level who find themselves giving their sons over to a bride that doesn't measure up or is not to their liking. Romans 8:28 is both a comfort and confidence to possess when walking down the aisle.

"And we know that God causes all things to work together for good to those who love God, to those who are called according to His purpose."

—Romans 8:28

"Peace I leave with you; My peace I give to you; not as the world gives do I give to you. Do not let your heart be troubled, nor let it be fearful."

≈John 14:27

July 17, 2019

There are not enough hours in the day. I'm sure you feel the same. Especially when it's been a good day like today was. I played in Eden's room for a good hour as she had me sitting in her closet while the pretend "storm" passed and she was tending to her hungry twins. She would run to her kitchen and prepare milk bottles for them. She even made pretend snacks and delivered it all so sweetly on plates, one to me and one to the twins. The snacks were apparently hot because she put socks on both hands so she wouldn't burn her hands from her oven. This pretend play went on for an hour, but I was enjoying myself so much and enjoying the quiet of the night and because my ears were not ringing it felt like maybe ten minutes had passed and then it was time for bed. Eden expressed my exact heart when she looked at me as if to cry and said, "Mama, I want to play all night." So I said, "Me too, me too Eden Joy, but God gives His beloved sleep."

Before we wrapped up for bed, I bought a few things from her store called "Eden's Joy." She checked me out and scanned the items that I purchased. I told her that I hadn't been somewhere with such fantastic service in a long time. She looked at me and smiled. She was really into it. I adored watching her hands grab the items and then scan them. It was amazing to me how careful she was with everything. She was so gentle with each item, carefully organizing where it went then putting it down gently. I could hear the noises of her plastic toys so clearly as she was setting them down. It was a peaceful time.

I love and appreciate good days. Especially since today, I found out that a friend that has been battling cancer for eight years by doing an all-natural cure is now losing the battle. It was hard to hear that. So today I was extra careful to enjoy it all. Thankfully the dear friend is a Christian, so her life is only about to begin when she dies. But still, it is hard.

Lord, life here is so short. Help all of us to redeem the time because the days are evil (Eph 5:16). Help us to be focused to share with the lost, to love our families well and neighbors and most of all You. Teach us to number our days that we might gain hearts of wisdom (Psalm 90:12). Amen.

Last Saturday, Eden looked at me and said, "Mama, I go where you go." That was incredibly sweet to hear. And now that I think about it, she may have gotten it from our time reading the book of Ruth when Ruth told Naomi something similar. I had just been reading the account to her I think the day before and she must have retained that one portion.

Scripture is designed to grab our attention that way. Eden consistently is engaged when I'm reading from her children's bible because someone is always getting hurt or is in trouble or there is evil around the corner, and she wants to find out what will happen. She seems always to perk up and pay extra attention when something goes wrong. That's true of open-air preaching too. A good heckler yelling at my husband, Emilio, will draw a crowd of 100 in a matter of minutes. I also find this to be true in our daily lives. There is not a day that goes by where I don't hear of some terrible thing that is going on whether it be a bad news report or a church member sick or something needing fixing at home or Eden falling and hurting herself or someone who was once beloved having left the faith. The list can go on but take heart friends. Jesus said, "In this world you will have many troubles; but be of good cheer I have overcome the world (John 16:33)." That is so true and so comforting all wrapped up in one warm blanket for us all to sleep in tonight.

"Peace I leave with you; My peace I give to you; not as the world gives do I give to you.
Do not let your heart be troubled, nor let it be fearful."

⸺John 14:27

CONTENTMENT

"…Be careful how you walk, not as unwise men but as wise."

Ephesians 5:15

July 18, 2019

Last night Eden woke up crying saying, "Mama can we just stay home?" Perhaps I've been running too many errands. On Sunday we were at church all day then went to Hat Creek Burger Company for dinner and got home late in the evening. On Monday we ran a few errands, but only made about four stops and they were quick. Eden slept in the car for two of the stops, and I stayed with her while Emilio went in to get groceries. Then yesterday I went to three locations: an ice cream store, Costco and Sprouts. We were only out a total of maybe two hours. I figure sometimes she might get bored at home, but she thinks differently than I do. I have a lot to learn from her. And now that I think about it, on Saturday we went to several places all practically in the same shopping strip. And I think instead of training her to be on the go I'd like to train her to be busy at home. I'm still trying to strike a balance between the two.

Then tonight before bed, she said again, "Mama, can we just stay home?" So tomorrow we will do that (as we did today) and I will try to play the audio bible, worship songs and just do a lot of reading and free play time. I felt like today, even though I was at home all day, I was on the phone working a bit more than I'd like. Tomorrow I want to slow down and breathe and feed the birds and wash Eden's hair (I always tell her I'm going to put a garden on her hair because this bottle of shampoo we have at home has pretty green flowers lining the bottom) and I'll clip her nails and maybe read *Miss Molly's School of Manners*. We also have been going through Eden's large Beginner's bible. It's about 500 pages long with not too many words and beautiful pictures on every page. We started reading page by page about ten days ago, and are about 75% done. I find that reading from front to back and having a "reading plan" is a good idea and helps us both see that we are making progress.

I also find that I'm always thinking of the next thing to do or where we will go next, but she doesn't think that way. She is fully present where she is; like the quote from Jim Elliot, "Wherever you are, be all there." And I certainly want her to be all there. I'm the one that needs to adapt and change and learn contentment. After all, we know that godliness coupled with contentment is great gain (1 Tim 6:6). At our first church plant in Keller, TX there was a sweet lady who had paid off her mortgage early and I asked her how she did it. I was really interested especially because that tends to be rare. She told me that she didn't go window shopping often. Because if she window shopped her eyes would covet and want something and then she would buy it. She managed to save a lot of money by refraining. Talk about contentment coupled with self-control. What a rare and wonderful combination.

Today I felt that I was fighting to be all there, wherever I was. I desire to be fully present, enjoying the task at hand, not having my mind elsewhere, unless it is in prayer or praise of course. It's a delicate balance, though. I'm not even sure if any of this is making sense. I also feel as if I wish I had ten hands to do more, but God gave me two, not ten. He wants me to do what two hands can do in a day and let the unfinished tasks rest at night. "Sufficient is the trouble for today," Matthew 6:34 says.

Perhaps a good verse for our souls to meditate and or memorize today is, "But godliness with contentment is great gain, for we brought nothing into the world, and we cannot take anything out of the world. But if we have food and clothing, with these we will be content" (1 Timothy 6:6-7).

Did you hear what you just read? With food and clothing, we shall be content. Boy oh boy, if we could truly live that way. We think we need so much more. Forgive me, Lord. Forgive us. Amen.

"…Be careful how you walk, not as unwise men but as wise."

Ephesians 5:15

"Serve the LORD with gladness; come into His presence with joyful songs."

Psalm 100:2

*J*uly 20, 2019

I have been doing a lot of cleaning lately, endeavoring to clean a drawer a day. Or every other day. And some days, like today and yesterday, I felt good and was able to clean four! It is amazing with how much you'll be able to gather to either throw away or give away or put in a better place so that it is more useful at home. A Victorian quote I read recently said, "A place for everything and everything in its place. I always put my things away, that I might find them another day." What a great saying for Eden to memorize. I might make it a jingle this week and try to put it into practice because for things to run smoothly, everything needs to have a home in the house. All our drawers, cabinets and closets are just smaller houses within a house if you will.

Or you can think of your home as a store. Imagine if every time you went shopping at Sprouts or Trader Joe's or Costco or Walmart, the items were shuffled around. You would never learn the store and would waste so much time. I'm sure you have your favorite stores that you've become so familiar with that you could work there or point people in the direction they would need to go should they ask you for help finding something. And our homes should be no different.

God calls us to be "keepers" of the home (Timothy 2:5), and the Proverbs 31 woman doesn't eat the bread of "idleness"

(Proverbs 31:27). The work of housekeeping is such a serious work that it can be a full-time job. At least that is what I have found. I want to aim this week to try to teach Eden this principle a bit more intentionally. Today I pulled out one large drawer to organize, and she got so into organizing it that it kept her entertained for a long time. So much so that I kept the drawer out in our front room and it's still there as I type.

Thank you, Lord, for the grace and strength you gave today to clean. Thank you that you are a God of order because if you ran the Universe the way I have kept my home the last two years, we all would be in big trouble. Amen.

"Serve the LORD with gladness; come into His presence with joyful songs."

Psalm 100:2

AWE

"...Weeping may last for the night, But a shout of joy comes in the morning."

—Psalm 30:5

July 23, 2019

I've had a lot of good days here recently and was able to clean and organize several things in the house. Like today, I cleaned the garage, a junk drawer, and Emilio's sock drawer. His sock drawer was no small feat (no pun intended) as he has more socks than anyone I've ever met. And I feared Eden would grow a year older before I finished organizing it. But God calls me to tend to him as well.

I also cleaned out our closet some and two bathroom drawers. I didn't tell Emilio about some of the detail work I'd done, and he may never notice, but God was watching. All this organizing reminds me again that being a keeper of the home can be a full-time job, but it feels good to do it. My mom came over tonight and told me she was doing the very same thing. Her home is neat and organized, and so is her purse. She always has a mint in there to give to Eden when she sees her. Eden will get one for me, and one for her, and I get to open them both. I'm sure I'll cry the day she opens them herself.

Speaking of crying, I'm holding Eden as I write and I cried hard over her (literally) as she fell asleep, for several reasons. One is that even though I was home with her all day, I felt like it wasn't enough time. We did read and color and run and sing and also went on a long walk and cleaned and read many stories from a new children's bible we bought her. But then she skipped a nap today and seemed like she still had a lot of energy. I missed the nap, but at least she wanted me to hold her for a bit. Some days she needs a nap and others she doesn't, so I'm still learning.

Like our walks with the Lord. We are always learning, and we find out that we never quite know as much as we thought we knew (Job 36:26). Our understanding of Him is a growing process. And we can be at church all day, being under the teaching of the Word and still feel as if it's not enough. We need to meet with the Lord for just a bit longer.

It reminds me of a time Emilio and I had missionary Josef Urban and his family over for a couple of days. All Emilio and Josef did, late into the evening, was talk about the Lord and theology. Then Emilio came into our room, plopped on the bed, opened his bible and took a deep sigh and said, "Awe." It struck a funny cord in my heart because he was acting as if he hadn't read the bible in days. He had just been talking about nothing but scripture for hours! That's what is wonderful about the Lord. He is limitless. We can't get enough of Him.

I also was crying because Eden is growing so fast (the story of my life). It's like I put her to bed and wonder if she will be the same child when I awake. And that is a painful thought. Thank God that He doesn't change when we wake up. He is the same yesterday, today and tomorrow, with new mercies to boot (Hebrews 13:8, Lamentations 3:22-23).

It dawned on me recently that Eden stopped carrying around one of her many stuffed animals up under her arm. May God resurrect that. She also has stopped yelling, "Maaaaaammmmaaaa!" as if to say, "Come in my room and play!" May God resurrect that too.

> *"…Weeping may last for the night, But a shout of joy comes in the morning."*
>
> ⸺Psalm 30:5

❧ DEPENDENCE ❧

"Let us hold resolutely to the hope we profess, for He who prom-ised is faithful."

═Hebrews 10:23

*J*uly 24, 2019

Tonight I'm doing so much better than yesterday. Last night I was crying and tonight I feel stronger by God's grace and thanking Him for a tangible sense of His mercies being new (Lam 3:23). It was also a good day with Eden. We ran to the 99 cent store and then to Hobby Lobby then to UPS and then to the Puppy store to pet the cats and then to Sprouts and finally Walmart. A few of the stores we were only there a few minutes. Then we got home today and played in her room and had snacks and went on a nice walk. We passed out a lot of tracts and Eden was even given the gift of a little bubble girl for free. I pulled down some boots that I bought her in California for her to try on for dress up and then she grabbed a rain jacket and wanted to wear it with. It was so sweet how she pieced it together. A part of me doesn't want to tell her the saying you did good "all on your own" because although it's true, I want her to see dependence as valuable as well. As we know folly is bound up in a child (Prov. 22:15) and nature has it (because of the fall) that when we are left to ourselves (Prov. 29:15) or we do things at times all on our own we can tend to get in trouble. Obviously I'm taking a small analogy to its ex-treme. But I'm trying to seek a balance of encouraging her to still depend on me and also praise her for growing and learn-ing new things on her own. Both dependence and growth are good and biblical. We are to depend (Psalm 62:5) on God and grow (2 Peter 3:18). I want to nurture both. I don't want her to think doing things all on her own is so great. Because we need each other and this is a biblical truth as well.

This all reminds me of the verse "A man who isolates himself seeks his own desire and rages against all wise counsel (Prov. 18:1). Remember in the book of Judges (when there was no king) the people did what was "right in their own eyes" (Judges 17:6) and they got into trouble. So I certainly want to praise her for doing things well and for progressing but I also want to build in her a constant or consistent acknowledgement of her parents as in permission to do things etc., and also praise her when she relies on us for things as well and perhaps then she will understand how to acknowledge God in all her ways (Prov. 3:5-6) and lean on Him just as she has been trained to include us in her daily activities and lean on us for help.

I could hear Eden down the hall this evening saying to one of her animals "the Word of God is living and active sharper than any two edge sword (Heb. 4:12)." I said a big "Amen" in my heart. So tonight before bed I quoted it back to her and she pretended to stab her side on the sharper than two edge sword part. Ahahaha she is really listening. She gets that from the story of when Saul try's to kill David with a sword. I have told her about that one a lot and she has pieced it all together. Thankfully God's Sword is a good one. To ward off the enemy and also to cut off any cancerous enemies that might grow in our hearts. As D. L. Moody once said "The Word will keep you from sin or sin will keep you from the Word."

Lord, protect Eden as she sleeps tonight. Protect her dreams. She woke up crying a bit ago. But not sure why so I just comforted her. Also on our walk tonight we talked about heaven. Eden out of the blue asked if David as in King David the Psalmist would be there. I said "Of course." Then I said and so will a bunch of others like Adam and Eve and Nahum and Zephaniah and Hagghi and Zachariah and Malachi. Also

Matthew, Mark, Luke and John. Now that I think about it if I wouldn't have mentioned Eve…Eden may have thought that heaven is just for men. Hahahah tomorrow maybe I will talk about Esther and Deborah and Mary (Jesus' mama) and Mary and Martha and Priscilla being there just to balance things out. I told her Judas won't be there and she said, "because he went to the pit." Exactly right, Eden! And what a thought we will never meet him. And aren't you glad?!

"Let us hold resolutely to the hope we profess, for He who promised is faithful."

Hebrews 10:23

❧ SENSITIVE ❧

"I will sing to the LORD as long as I live;
I will sing praise to my God while I have my being."

—Psalm 104:33

*J*uly 27, 2019

There is a particular prayer that I have prayed many times, and must pray again tonight, as I hear of so many that were in the faith falling away. My prayer is this,

> *"God, please help Eden not to be a false convert. I'm teaching her a lot of Your Word, please allow it to work for good as I have Your promise that it will not come back void (Isa 55:11). Eden seems to have a tender heart right now, even tender towards loud noises. Like she told me today that she will never like loud cars or motorcycles. And she was digging through some toys in the garage, and I thought she knew I was closing the garage door, but it startled her, and she cried and cried. I comforted her, and we went back to play. I pray, Lord, in the same way that she is sensitive to loud noises, that she will be sensitive to the prompting and leading of your Spirit. Please cause her to have genuine salvation. And for her to have an assurance that You love her. Lord, thank you for purging Your Church. It's hard to see people fall away, and it causes us to ache. But You are not surprised or moved by any of this. All glory be to Your name, Amen."*

After hearing of an influential leader in Christianity falling away, I thought of the song lyrics, "Though none go with me, still I will follow." I can sing that with truth and mean it, but I do pray that Eden will go with me and that she will have a place at the banqueting table. She has told me several times that she doesn't want to go to the pit. I thank God for this.

I played Matt Redman's song "10,000 Reasons" on the piano, and Eden sang along and rocked in a little rocking chair. I'm amazed that she knows a large portion of the song, and after we sang together, she had the song on her lips for a good part of the evening. Music is a powerful tool for learning. Let us be intentional with what the little ears around us hear in our homes.

"I will sing to the LORD as long as I live;
I will sing praise to my God while I have my being."

⹀Psalm 104:33

"Let us not neglect assembling together…"

⇌Hebrews 10:25

*J*uly 29, 2019

Today was an excellent day at church. The church felt full as we sang "What can wash away my sins? Nothing but the blood of Jesus!" Eden sang too and seemed to be really trying to sing on key.

Then Emilio began his preaching through the book of Isaiah, which has turned out to be very edifying. I had Eden listen carefully and whisper to me if she heard a word she knew, and then I would write it down in her coloring book. We ended up with about 40 words. Words like unbelievers, Isaiah, God, walk, walking, and redeemer. It was fun. A few words she said rather loudly, perhaps out of excitement at hearing a word she knew, so I had to remind her to whisper. She typically does very well in service. It's a delight to my heart to have her by my knees standing. I love being able to listen to the sermon and watch her color or draw or enjoy the message.

We also had a big family visit our church today. They have been listening to Emilio's sermons for three years and had been praying about leaving their church to come to ours. You just never know who is listening. This new family is dear, and I pray they stay as we just had a big family leave our church because of work relocation.

A sweet ending to today was Eden singing the entire Lord's Prayer before bed. She sang it three times. I was blessed by it even though her theology was off. She kept singing, "My will be done" instead of "Thy." "My" and "thy" sound so similar, but they're worlds apart in meaning. May God help our children to one day to understand the difference when they sing "Thy will be done."

"Let us not neglect assembling together..."

Hebrews 10:25

Remedy

"The LORD is good, A stronghold in the day of trouble, and He knows those who trust in Him."

—Nahum 1:7

July 30, 2019

I was a bit down today, not because of my health, which was good, but because of Eden's sour attitude. I'm certain lack of sleep was a key culprit. Last week she went to bed early, no problem. This week she didn't want to go down so easily. So today I had to be on guard. On my to-do list was to run to the UPS store, which is minutes from my home, so we did, and I'm glad we did because the Marble Slab ice cream store right next to it was calling our names. I thought that perhaps God could use it to brighten things up. Of course, I can't eat anything there because of my thyroid and autoimmune condition, but I thought I would get Eden the smallest ice cream they had. She told me she wanted to try the green one. It was mint. Then she wanted to try strawberry, and she told me she wanted mint because it tasted like Meesie's (my mom's) mints. So I bought it and gave the young girl working a tract for the Unpopular movie.

Minutes later, a lady came in and said: "Is that your car outside running?" I said, "Yes, ma'am, it sure is." Then she said, "My daughter needs help with her dog. Can I have a card?"

We have magnetic signs on my SUV advertising our dog business, www.dfwdogwhisperers.com. The lady said, "Your car was in the right place at the right time." Amen to that. I gave her a gospel tract too, and said something like, "This is probably the real reason you came in." She was grateful. May God save her whole family.

Then the young girl behind the ice cream counter said, "You are popular." I wasn't sure what she said as I was thinking she was referring to our film "Unpopular," so I said, "I'm sorry, what did you say?" She said that the lady recognized me and I must be popular, referring to our movie, not my car with the dog magnets on it. Too funny. I forget what I said but next time, I'll say something like, "No. Our film isn't all that popular and some don't like the message in it at all hahah but others love it, you'll have to judge for yourself."

Eden and I moved outside to finish eating the rest of the ice-cream, and within a few minutes time passed out several tracts to people who thought Eden "looked cute." Then we heard a car crash somewhere near. And saw a lady taking her sick dog into the veterinarian's office next door. Both reminders of how broken our world is. So I sang a song called, "Is He Worthy",

"Do you feel the world is broken? We do.

Do you feel the shadows deepen? We do."

It's actually a hopeful song. It talks about how the world is broken and that Jesus is the remedy. It's a soul strengthening song for when we hear cars crash and see sickness in our midst, and so is scripture. Eden quoted today, "The Lord is close to the brokenhearted and saves those who are crushed in spirit." It's wonderful that she has scripture memorized and can quote it to herself and me.

Are you feeling broken today, dear reader? Are you feeling crushed in spirit? Well, you have God's word that He is close. Did you hear that? He is close. Let me repeat it. He is close. To the brokenhearted. And he will save those who are crushed in spirit. Praise be to God.

"The LORD is good, A stronghold in the day of trouble, and He knows those who trust in Him."

⇒Nahum 1:7

CALLED

"Blessed are those who do His commandments, that they may have the right to the tree of life, and may enter through the gates into the city."

Revelation 22:14

July 31, 2019

On Sunday Eden and I wore matching all-white dresses to church. The book of Revelation speaks of the bride of Christ being dressed in white. I'm in Christ, and I pray Eden will be too one day.

Tonight before bed and after a bath I held Eden in my arms and wrapped her in the towel as she rested her head on my shoulder while I danced with her to the old DC Talk song "I Want To Be In The Light." I told her that it was one of my favorite songs from when I first got saved. I'm so thankful to my high school friend that challenged me to listen to nothing but Air 1 Christian Radio for one week. I took her up on that, and never went back to the world for music. I remember listening and crying in my car at Baseline Road and Haven Avenue in Rancho Cucamonga, CA. I have my mom and stepdad, to thank as well, as they prayed fervently for my salvation. Years after becoming a Christian, I learned that my stepdad, Mike, was faithfully in his room on his knees praying for me. He prayed for me, not because I was a troubled kid, I got excellent grades, but because my soul was in trouble. I hardly ever missed a day of school too, but inwardly I was doing it all for my name and to please man and just because I didn't want to miss out on the activities of the day.

There was, however, a drawing of the Lord in my early years. Early awakenings to the things of God, which He used to spare me of drugs and smoking and things like that. But it wasn't until my junior year in high school that I would stumble upon Ephesians 5 in my bed one night, thoroughly convicted that I was the sinner it described. It was that night that I repented, and a holy dread of judgment came upon me. It was as if the Lord was saying, "Today is the day to lay it all down," and every competitor for the Lord and His love was instantly unsatisfying. That was the night it all began for me. I thought I had chosen Him, but He chose me. I sincerely thought I had been the one that first loved Him, but He was the one awakening my sinful heart and then effectually calling me to Himself. I would not have been able to articulate that to you quite like that at the time. I just knew I was blind and then I could see. I knew that the Bible knew me better than I knew me. It was written so long ago, but knew my heart. Praise God!

Several times through the day Eden told me that she loved me. I don't tire from hearing it, and I always am a bit surprised when she says it. Like I wonder, how do I deserve the love of such a dear person?

I also don't tire from praying for her salvation. Out of the blue, she said to me, "Oh mama, I don't want you to go to the pit." I laughed and told her I wasn't going to the pit because I'm a Christian. At least she is thinking of spiritual things. As much as I ache over her growth, I know that growth is good so that she can one day have a clear understanding of the Gospel. The verses that we have been memorizing and meditating on this week to help her with that are,

> "The wages of sin is death, but the gift of God is eternal life in Christ Jesus." (Romans 6:23)

And, "Then Jesus again spoke to them, saying, 'I am the Light of the world; he who follows Me will not walk in the darkness, but will have the Light of life.'" (John 8:12)

A friend from church sent a video of her little daughter singing a tune she made up to Romans 6:23. I play it over and over on my phone for Eden. We also sing and do hand movements to a song by Seeds Family Worship for John 8:12. I had prayed on Sunday that we could find new songs to sing and new verses to memorize this week. I see that prayer being answered and it's only Wednesday.

Lord, put new tunes and songs in our hearts that we may praise you all our days. Turn our mourning into dancing. Amen.

Revelation 5:9 says,

> *"And they sang a new song: "Worthy are You to take the scroll and open its seals, because You were slain, and by Your blood You purchased for God those from every tribe and tongue and people and nation."*

Psalm 28:7 *"The LORD is my strength and my shield; my heart trusts in Him, and I am helped. Therefore my heart rejoices, and I will thank Him with my song."*

Psalm 30:11 *"You have turned for me my mourning into dancing; You have loosed my sackcloth and girded me with gladness."*

Psalm 32:7 *"You are my hiding place. You protect me from trouble; You surround me with songs of deliverance. Selah"*

Psalm 33:3 *"Sing to Him a new song; play skillfully with a shout of joy."*

Psalm 96:1 *"Sing to the LORD a new song; sing to the LORD, all the earth."*

Psalm 144:9 *"I will sing to You a new song, O God; on a harp of ten strings I will make music to You,"*

Isaiah 42:10 *"Sing to the LORD a new song, His praise from the ends of the earth, you who go down to the sea, and all that is in it, you islands, and all who dwell there."*

> *"Blessed are those who do His commandments, that they may have the right to the tree of life, and may enter through the gates into the city."*
>
> ⇋Revelation 22:14

⤙ CORRECTION ⤚

"Be diligent to present yourself approved to God as a workman who does not need to be ashamed, accurately handling the word of truth."

⇒2 Timothy 2:15

*A*ugust 1, 2019

Eden mispronounces some words. And it's so cute I can't correct her. She says, "Libraryia" for "library" and "soon" for "spoon" and "gadness" for "gladness." It reminds me a bit of how the Lord was patient with us in correcting our theology. Not that He thought our error was cute, but He was simply gentle and patient with us. At least I can testify to that as it took me a long time for my thinking and even speech to be corrected from the Word of Faith movement. My theology was off, but as I studied and grew, it has become stronger and more clearly defined in truth. As Eden grows, no doubt her language will do the same.

"Be diligent to present yourself approved to God as a workman who does not need to be ashamed, accurately handling the word of truth."

—2 Timothy 2:15

⤙ LIGHT ⤚

*A*ugust 2, 2019

I have a giant print bible that a person I've never met shipped to me. Karen is a Wretched Radio listener (the ministry I used to work for) and has become dear to me. All just by sending me messages on Facebook. I guess she has become a modern-day pen pal.

I read the bible she sent me a lot when Eden was first born up until she was around one year old, and then I began reading other bibles. Tonight I decided to pick it back up, and since God is a God of order, I thought I should become a bit more orderly in my bible reading. So I started reading at the beginning (literally) in Genesis 1, and I found that I could not get past Genesis 3. There is just so much in those first chapters; it's hard to move on.

There were a couple of insights that struck me. One is that God must love light. It is one of the very first things He mentions in Genesis chapter 1. In fact, He is light (1 John 1:5). And Revelation 21:23 talks about how in heaven, we will need no light at all because He will be the light and the Lamb (Jesus) will be the lamp.

The first thing God did on day 1 was say, "Let there be light, and there was light." On day 4, he creates the sun and the moon. I immediately thought that He must not like darkness, so it's okay for us to have night lights on, even as adults, in our home. It sounds funny, but for fun, my mom spent the night last Saturday and stayed in Eden's room. She brought her blow-up bed and everything. As I was making sure the house was in order before bed, I walked down the hall and noticed she had left on a night light. I chuckled as I do the same thing. I always have. And God hung his night light (the moon) for us at night. Can you imagine if we didn't have it? I wanted to sleep with a light on as a kid, and I still do. Not quite as bright now as it was back then, but it's light nonetheless. If any of you feel silly for ever using night lights, well, let me free you with this one verse... "Be dressed in readiness and keep your lamps lit." (Luke 12:35)

The other insight I had was Adam and Eve realizing they were naked. It made me think of Eden, who is so unaware of whether she is clothed or not clothed. She doesn't have a care about that right now. She pays no mind to her body except to complain if her diaper is falling off or her pants are too tight or her dress is uncomfortable, but the innocence of her naked-ness reminded me of Adam and Eve. Perhaps they had that sort of innocence, but then sin entered in, and they were well aware of themselves. In a way, I must confess, I'm dreading Eden realizing these things. I want her just to stay as she is, but it's not God's will. Adam and Eve's sin is the reason God clothed them with animal skins, which was pointing to the Lamb of God (Jesus) that we must be clothed with. So when that time comes when Eden is ashamed of her nakedness, maybe it won't be so bad after all because I will be able to talk about how Adam and Eve felt that way too and the reason she feels it is because of sin. I'll tell her that in heaven we will be clothed. We won't be naked. So in God's great plan, nakedness is not the most innocent thing after all. The most innocent thing is being clothed in white robes. How wonderful.

> After these things I looked, and behold, a great multi-tude which no one could count, from every nation and all tribes and peoples and tongues, standing before the throne and before the Lamb, clothed in white robes,

and palm branches were in their hands; and they cry out with a loud voice, saying,

"Salvation to our God,

who sits on the throne, and to the Lamb."

And all the angels were standing around the throne and around the elders and the four living creatures; and they fell on their faces before the throne and worshiped God, saying,

"Amen,

blessing and glory

and wisdom and thanksgiving and honor

and power and might, be to our God forever and ever.

Amen."

Then one of the elders answered, saying to me, "These who are clothed in the white robes, who are they, and where have they come from?"

I said to him, "My lord, you know."

And he said to me, "These are the ones who come out of the great tribulation, and they have washed their robes and made them white in the blood of the Lamb.

"For this reason, they are before the throne of God;

and they serve Him day and night in His temple;

and He who sits on the throne will spread His tabernacle over them.

"They will hunger no longer,

nor thirst anymore;

nor will the sun beat down on them, nor any heat;

for the Lamb in the center of the throne will be their shepherd,

and will guide them to springs of the water of life;

and God will wipe every tear from their eyes." ~Revelation 7:9–17

"Bless the LORD, O my soul, and all that is within me, bless His holy name."

➤Psalm 103:1

⤚⚬ STRENGTH ⚬⤚

"Naked I came from my mother's womb, And naked I shall return there."

⇒Job 1:21

*A*ugust 3, 2019

Today Eden and I talked a lot about the Bible. We finished reading her Beginner's Bible and have moved on to a bit of a larger one. She was eager to hear the story of Dagon the false God found in 1 Samuel 5, especially the part where he repeatedly fell on his face before the ark of the Lord. She also liked the account of Gideon, who felt his army was too small to defeat God's enemy. God told him that his army was actually too large and said, "Tell the men that are afraid to go home." Gideon agreed to do that since fearful men are of no use in battle, and many men left.

God then tells Gideon to have his men drink from a spring saying, "You shall separate everyone who laps the water with his tongue as a dog laps, as well as everyone who kneels to drink. 300 men lapped the water like a dog, while many more kneeled, but God wanted the glory so Gideon went to battle with only the 300. God wanted to win the fight, so that it was all Him and no boasting of man.

This account makes me think of Noah, who could not boast that he saved himself from the floodwaters; it was all of God using the ark to do the saving work. God even told him how to build the ark. Just like salvation, we can't boast in saving ourselves. Rather, God sent Jesus (the ultimate ark) to save us from our sins. And look at David, he was so small (so small the regular sized armor would not even fit him), but he had a giant God to defeat Goliath.

Then we talked about Samson. Eden really wanted to talk a lot about his hair getting cut off. It's good to know his strength was not in his hair, but in the God who gave him his hair. This will be a comfort to me when the day comes that I have to cut Eden's hair. I've never put scissors to her hair, and can't even bear the thought. Lord, thank you that our strength is not in our wisdom, our money, our possessions, in who we know or don't know, in our jobs, in our families or our children (though we like those things and thank you for them), but our strength and breath and life are found in You alone.

Random thought, I've quoted this verse from Acts 20:35 to Eden several times lately, "It's better to give than to receive." I'm not sure she understands it, but that's okay. And truth is I don't think I do either. For example, possessions tend to be easy for me to give away, but people I love, not so much. For example, I don't look forward to the day we have to give Eden away in marriage. Perhaps this verse applies to that situation too. I have to trust that God's Word is true and wiser than I am. He says it is "better to give" and He doesn't lie and He will show us how it is so, whether here on earth or in Heaven.

Lord, I pray for all the dear readers that have had to give, give, give and give some more. You know how to give Lord, as you are the inventor of it. It's the path to life because you gave your Son so that we could have eternal life. And Lord all things on this earth must be given away so that we can gain eternal pleasures at your right hand forever more (Psalm 16:11). Amen.

"Naked I came from my mother's womb, And naked I shall return there."

⟣Job 1:21

⤜◆ HEAVEN ◆⤛

"Set your minds on things above, not on earthly things."

⤜Colossians 3:2

ugust 4, 2019

We've had a lot of fun recently with Eden's preschool papers. I hang them up on my blinds like curtains. Soon I'll have real curtains as Eden's "Nana" (my aunt) ordered some to blackout the sun, but it seems like the Lord will come back before they arrive. It will be worth the wait though, and I'll be incredibly grateful to not have to my nightly ritual of hanging up the black tablecloths I purchased from the Dollar Store. That's something to look forward to.

Something else we're looking forward to is tomorrow night's family dinner for Emilio's birthday. I've been coming up with questions for everyone to talk about around the table. My favorite so far is, "What sort of things will we not do in heaven?"

I've come up with a few things, and I'm excited to see what the others come up with. Here's my list:

1. Lock the doors
2. Go potty or wear diapers (Eden will like this)
3. Fly in airplanes or drive cars
4. Bathe or shower (I suppose)
5. Change light bulbs
6. Sleep
7. Sin

8. Witness or tell others to repent (everyone there will know the Lord)

9. Cry or mourn (unless tears of joy)

10. Die or fear death

11. Long to be with the Lord. That's the ultimate thing to look forward to!

"Set your minds on things above, not on earthly things."

Colossians 3:2

~⊙ TOGETHERNESS ⊙~

"In all your ways acknowledge Him, And He will make your paths straight."

≡Proverbs 3:6

*A*ugust 7, 2019

Eden peeked into my closet and said to me, "I go wherever you go." It's a line that Ruth told Naomi in the Bible. It was Ruth's way of saying, "I will follow you, Naomi, and serve your God." And may it be a line that Eden will continue to tell me all her days. I desire for her not to go off to college or to leave home like that, but perhaps instead run a local small business or assist in ministry or be a stay-at-home mom (after she marries a Christian man that lives in our town, of course!) I'm not sure if this is God's will for her, but I can pray it is and I know God hears so we will see.

I walked into the living room where Emilio was watching an episode of Shark Tank. A mom and daughter were on showing their invention that had taken off and made them millions. They seemed very close and very loving to each other as they were arm-in-arm and the daughter was crying tears of gratitude. The honor and respect between the two of them was touching so I prayed a secret prayer in my heart that Eden and I could be like that. Maybe we won't be millionaires, but I hope our relationship will reap millions in eternity together, as in millions of souls that we can labor together in God's field. That would be worth more than any amount of money made on earth.

I'm also touched by a family in our church that I've known for close to twenty years. They left California to move to Texas around the same time Emilio and I did to attend our church. Recently, their oldest daughter got married and moved about a block away from them with her new husband, Julio. They had a baby within their first year of marriage, and she sees her mom almost daily, if not daily. I have prayed many nights that Eden will marry a man similar to Julio in that he will love the Lord, serve at our church, be a hard worker, desire to have children quickly, so I can hold them (Ha!) and we can have wonderful family time together. What a joy and delight that would be. And of course, I pray Eden's husband will have a heart for the lost and be as close to perfect as possible. Amen. That was sort of like a prayer so I'll add another Amen.

"In all your ways acknowledge Him, And He will make your paths straight."

Proverbs 3:6

"A merry heart does like good medicine...."

Proverbs 17:22

August 9, 2019

Today at Costco, upon checking out, I could not get over how fast the three workers swarmed my shopping cart to get out about 10 items. Eden was sitting in the cart, and she almost started crying from how fast they approached. Some things in my cart belong to my mom, who was shopping with us, and they took those too. I didn't even have time to think, let alone speak. It was as if they were on energy drinks or on high-speed Internet mode.

Then we went to get food from the food court, and they worked just as fast there. Perhaps I'm getting old and slowing down a bit, or maybe Eden has taught me to stop and smell the flowers a bit more, which is good because sometimes I feel that I'm often in warp speed (for all the Star Wars fans out there). And when you are in that mode, you can miss out on so much. It's like eating a 5-star meal while standing up. It's hard to savor food like that. Something about sitting to eat helps you to really taste. And the same is true with the Lord; we need to "taste and see that the Lord is good" (Psalm 34:8). But sometimes that kind of tasting takes time. This week for nearly five days Eden and I meditated on just three verses (all to song):

"For He satisfies the longing soul, and He fills the hungry soul with good things." -Psalm 107:9

"O come let us sing for joy to the Lord, let us shout joyfully to the God of our salvation." -Psalm 95:1

"For the wages of sin is death but the free gift of God is eternal life in Christ Jesus our Lord." -Romans 6:23

Taking longer to meditate on Scripture is beneficial as it allows God to do a work in us. Being in high-speed mode can cause us to be in the flesh, at least it can with me. Doing things slower or eliminating tasks from our list can also help us not be tempted to sin because "we are doing something, and we don't want anyone getting in our way, and we need to get our list done now!"

Tonight before bed, I happened upon a little video done by of a friend of mine, Maureen, that is dying from lung cancer and has been given about six months or less to live. I bet in many ways, she has slowed way down so that time can seem to move slower. Do you notice if you slow down things seem to take longer? So, if you want to savor time, slow down.

Maureen lives in California and is a pastor's wife. In the video, she's talking about a simple verse in 1 Corinthians 13 that talks about how "love is patient...love is kind." We all know the verse and can quote it, I'm sure. But she was talking about how if we are patient with people at our place of work or with our children or spouse, it will produce kindness. Consequently, if we are genuinely kind to people, it will produce patience.

She went on to talk about how sometimes we need to slow down, and that she has noticed that people tend not to be irritable on vacation because they have done just that. This made me laugh because she was filming her little short two-minute video as she was seemingly taking it easy on a cruise ship. She seemed so relaxed that you'd never know she was even sick, let alone had months to live. But she is sick, and though her voice sounded weak, her words were powerful. I listened to the video clip three times, and I'm so glad she slowed down enough to film it. I like what the Lord said in Isaiah 30:15 "For thus the Lord GOD, the Holy One of Israel, has said, 'In repentance and rest you will be saved, In quietness and trust is your strength.'" May God make us willing to rest. And may God help our children to be balanced in this high-speed world.

Psalm 95:1, "O come, let us sing unto the LORD: let us make a joyful noise to the rock of our salvation."

Hosea 6:1, "Come, and let us return unto the LORD: for he hath torn, and he will heal us; he hath smitten, and he will bind us up."

Psalm 95:6, "Come, let us worship and bow down: let us kneel before the LORD our maker."

Tonight I also got a crazy idea. I decided to try to start painting Eden's school room (so much for slowing down). We bought paint and supplies yesterday. I affectionately named the room, "Ma T's School of Manners, Learning and Biblical Education." Eden kicked the project off by painting some herself. It turned out to be a lot of fun and somewhat relaxing. We painted a cross on the wall and then a heart and then the words "Jesus' School Room." I want everything in that room to be done to the glory of God. I knew we had started things off on the right foot when Eden took her hand and squeezed the roller and paint dripped all on the carpet...and on her right foot.

"A merry heart does like good medicine...."

⸺Proverbs 17:22

⚬ CHILDLIKENESS ⚬

"A Psalm of David. The earth is the LORD'S, and all it contains, The world, and those who dwell in it."

⚬Psalm 24:1

*A*ugust 10, 2019

I felt particularly weak today. Like I wanted to cry five different times just because of my love for Eden. I wish I could tell her just how much I love her. I feel the same for my mom and all she has done for me. There is not enough time or days, though. I imagine the Lord is the same except He has given us a lot of words so that we can know. Sadly, many of His children don't treasure His words enough, and His love book collects dust. May this not be said of our children or us.

I went outside in God's creation and felt so much better. It was only 15 minutes at the park, but it did something to both Eden's mindset and mine. Eden went on the swing, and we watched the sunset. Perhaps if you feel in a rut or just a bit down, go outside and look at God's creation. Let your feet touch His grass and breathe in deeply His air.

Eden was very baby-like today, which also made me want to cry. When we are childlike, I can imagine it brings joy to the heart of our Lord. He wanted children near him (Matthew 19:14). And He has made it clear that those who are childlike in faith will enter into heaven.

I've noticed there is something special about Down syndrome children. They retain their childlikeness no matter their age. I have a vivid memory of going to eat when Eden was only about six months old. We were at Legacy West (a beautiful outdoor mall), and an adult Down syndrome man was eating next to us. He was so dear as he delighted in his food like no one else there. He was saying hello to everyone, and he seemed to have a permanent smile on his face. I got teary-eyed at the table while watching him glory in things. I gave him and his father a gospel tract before we left. May I see them again at another wonderful meal called "The Marriage Supper." Eden was too young to remember any of it. But maybe she will get to hear it all around the Marriage Supper table. What a wonderful thought.

Lord, only You can make things like this happen. Thank you that grateful people will be in heaven; people who are childlike and innocent. Amen.

"A Psalm of David. The earth is the LORD'S, and all it contains, The world, and those who dwell in it."

═Psalm 24:1

❧ PRIORITIES ❧

"Be anxious for nothing, but in everything by prayer and supplication with thanksgiving let your requests be made known to God."

— Philippians 4:6

August 11, 2019

A couple weeks ago I took on some work that I thought would be easy but turned out to be more than I bargained for. It was for a friend that I truly wanted to help, but as I sat back and re-evaluated, I realized the stress and pressure of it all was stealing my joy and my focus. I was so consumed with trying to figure out how to get the job done that it was robbing my time with Eden, and when I was with her, my mind was elsewhere. I found I was often in the flesh because of it. So I had to make the painful phone call to say I could not help. I cried hard after I hung up the phone because I hate having my yes be a no. I really try to keep my word. In fact, when I worked at Living Waters, I said yes to every new project that came my way, even if I had no idea how to do it. That was before I had Eden.

Now my thinking has changed, and so have my priorities. And I have realized that since time and money are fleeting, I'd rather try to conserve the time I have by not being irritable (which can be so easy) and by not giving in to the flesh (which also can be so easy), and try to eliminate anything that is a stumbling block. I have to face the fact that it's okay to say no sometimes and not save the world (since that is God's job anyway).

Lord, let Eden's best memories be of those in our home. Help my readers to evaluate their daily lives and see if any pressures perhaps can be removed so that they can free their minds up to serve their families and You better. Amen.

"Be anxious for nothing, but in everything by prayer and supplication with thanksgiving let your requests be made known to God."

〓Philippians 4:6

⤙ SEEK ⤚

*A*ugust 12, 2019

I managed to have a little more order today, and I'm glad for it. I found Eden was less irritable as boredom can make you grumpy. So we did our very first piano lesson at Ma T's School, and guitar lesson too. Her stuffed cat was my pupil, also. Then we got snacks and made gluten-free dairy-free cupcakes with chocolate chips. After that, we played seek and find in the back yard, and I told Eden that God says if we seek Him, we will find Him (Jeremiah 29:13).

Children love to seek and find. Perhaps God designed it that way just so we can teach them that verse. Eden found much more than I expected too. One thing was a ladybug that was no longer living. She asked me, "Will it eat my bunny crackers?"

"No," I said.

"Will it fly?

"No."

"Is it dead?" She inquired, as she squinted her eyes, and looked at me.

I was surprised by this question because I had not told her that, but answered, "Yes."

Later, it was bath time and Eden broke out in song singing,

"Victory in Jesus my Savior forever.

He bought me and sought me with His redeeming blood."

And a Chris Tomlin song,

"The God of angel armies

Is always by my side

The One who reigns forever

He is a friend of mine

Nothing formed against me shall stand

God holds the whole world in his hands."

Even little ladybugs. That's the God we serve.

"No weapon that is formed against you will prosper; And every tongue that accuses you in judgment you will condemn. This is the heritage of the servants of the LORD, And their vindication is from Me," declares the LORD."

⸗Isaiah 54:17

⤙ BATTLES ⤚

"A man's heart plans his course, but the LORD determines his steps."

⟺Proverbs 16:9

*A*ugust 13, 2019

If you find that you still battle daily with some sort of sin, such as impatience, lack of love, lack of kindness, lack of self-control or whatever it may be, welcome to the club. Remember, we are not perfected yet. I can tend to think that my day will go perfectly or that I will be the perfect mom, or at least try to aim for that, and fail to rely on the grace of God. I need to remind myself daily that I am not in my renewed body yet. We all know we are still going to battle sin, but sometimes we can think differently. I don't know about you, but if I stumble in one of these areas, I tend to beat myself up over it for hours. Not a constant beating up, but an intermittent sneaking in that robs me of precious time.

I think what is healthier and biblical is for us to think of our falling short like when a toddler actually falls. They don't allow it to consume their whole day, let alone their entire life. Instead, they get back up and move on after a quick cry and start playing again. We have a lot to learn from toddlers and children. Imagine if every time a toddler fell, they never wanted to try walking again. That would be silly. But somehow, as Christians, we tend to believe that we're going to have perfect days without any sort of internal or external struggle, which is just setting ourselves up for failure. What is best is to accept the grace of God quickly and let Him pick us up; keep short accounts with God daily and move on walking in joy and trusting that 1 John 1:9 is true.

"For a righteous man falls seven times, and rises again, But the wicked stumble in time of calamity." ~*Proverbs 24:16*

Thinking of keeping short accounts with God reminds me that it's essential for me to keep short accounts with Eden too. If I sense her behavior is off, I should deal with it quickly, so the behavior doesn't linger. Lingering issues can steal so much focus, time, and joy.

The song "Lord I need You" came onto the radio and we started singing, "Lord I need You, oh, I need You.

Every hour I need You.

My one defense my righteousness,

Oh, God, how I need you."

Eden closed her eyes and really seemed to sing from the heart.

Later that night, Eden took out her baby dolls, which up until now she has been clear about not being a fan of, and said: "I'm changing my heart about them."

"A man's heart plans his course, but the LORD determines his steps."

Proverbs 16:9

⋙ SWORD ⋘

*A*ugust 14, 2019

Eden said last night while playing, "Mama I can hear the scoffers beating somebody up. Tell them the Lord wants them to serve Him and to repent." To which I said a big hearty, "AMEN!" She was remembering The Good Samaritan from the Bible and a little cartoon of the account from The Beginner's Bible Series. I always tell her that the men who hurt that man were scoffers and The Good Samaritan was not a scoffer. We haven't watched the cartoon or read the story in a while, so it was neat to see the concept had stuck with her. We've also memorized Psalm 1, which talks about the blessed man not sitting in the seat of scoffers. I so pray Eden will be like that godly person that will not tolerate the wicked nor stand in the path of sinners nor sit in the seat of scoffers, but her delight will be in the law of the Lord and in His law she will meditate day and night, so that she will be like a tree firmly planted by streams of water whose leaf will not wither and in whatever she does will prosper. Amen.

That's a warning for us moms too. If you feel withered, then spend some time drinking from the Word. Your heart will be revived and come alive because:

"The Word of God is living and active sharper than any two-edged sword."

⋙ Hebrews 4:12

⤙ TEACHING ⤚

ugust 16, 2019

Can you spot my bad teaching? I was telling Eden that Noah broke the Ten Commandments in his sin when he came down from the mountain when she said, "No, it was NOT Noah! It was Moses!" I wasn't thinking, apparently. I better watch my theology around her.

"Be doers of the word, and not hearers only..."

⩦James 1:22

⌒ HANDS ⌒

"Therefore I urge you, brethren, by the mercies of God, to present your bodies a living and holy sacrifice, acceptable to God, which is your spiritual service of worship."

⌒Romans 12:1

*A*ugust 17, 2019

Something struck me about Noah that gave me an idea. I think I'll have Eden draw an outline of her hands, and ask her, "Did Noah use his hands for good?" And tell her, "Yes, he did. He built the Ark the way God designed it, but just imagine if he did his own thing. The Ark would have surely sunk." Then I can draw funny, exaggerated pictures of the Ark sinking to make her laugh. The same is true with us, especially if we try to parent the way we think we should instead of using God's manual (the Bible). We will sink in trouble.

Then I'll ask her who else in the bible used their hands for good? The answer is many. Mary did; she nurtured and cared for Jesus. Esther did; she helped to be a conduit to save her people. Same with Joseph and David and Abel and the prophets and of course the Lord Jesus. And I will ask her who used their hands for evil? Answer: Goliath and Cain and Delilah and Judas and Herod and Demas. And then I will ask her if she wants to use her hands for good or evil?

Speaking of that, tonight before bed, I asked her if she wanted to be a Christian, and she said yes. I said do you want to be used for good or evil? "Good," she said. On our nightly walk earlier tonight, I asked her if she could get to heaven by being a good person or with a ladder or by an airplane? To which she answered no to everything. And she said, "An airplane can only take us to The Wee Loft, silly!" I knew exactly what she meant, which is that an airplane can't take us to heaven, but it can take us to California where "The Wee Loft" toy store is. So, I said, "I'm confused...so...how do I get to heaven?" She said, "Can you tell me?" I love it when she says that. So I did. I told her through Jesus. By the cross. Through His death, burial and resurrection. Then we continued our walk. It was beautiful, and we sang as we went, enjoying the night. I'm sure we looked strange, not because we were singing, but because it was 90 degrees and I was wearing a sauna suit Emilio bought for me to sweat out impurities. But it works, and when we got home, Eden said, "Where did all that water come from?"

Side note for any thyroid sufferers like me: Studies show that saunas and things like that can help reduce fatigue symptoms and help you sleep better. I must say the first time I tried it I dreamed that I was having another child and we were telling our family. Then we were being attacked from above by airplanes. So, I'm not sure if I recommend the sauna suit just yet. But I have been able to eliminate my fatigue symptoms mostly and still have my medicine low (what I consider low at 50mg, considering at one point it was as high as 88mg) all through diet and lots of prayer. A typical meal consists of something like one of these:

Example Meal #1

Carrots, zucchini, chicken in coconut oil (all steamed on the stove) with potatoes or sweet potatoes.

Example Meal #2

Gluten-free lentil spaghetti with tomato sauce and a bunch of grilled mushrooms cooked in coconut oil with grilled spinach and gluten free bread.

Example Meal #2

Salmon with fresh vegetables and rice in coconut oil.

Snacks are things like:

> Turkey meat with sweet potato crackers and half avocado with salt.

> Almond milk heated with honey and cinnamon for a nice hot drink

Oh, and I eat a lot of fruit and juice them, sometimes daily with fresh organic pineapple, one orange, and one apple. It's delicious. Eden loves it, and it's frothy. You can throw cucumber and carrots in there too.

Be very careful with juicing kale and spinach and carrots and celery. These things can make you hyperthyroid and give you high heart rate coupled with anxiety.

And smoothies for meal replacements, here is what I make:

- Peanut butter 1T
- 1T protein powder
- 2T spinach (which you can freeze by the way) just add a handful.
- Nut milk (like almond milk or cashew milk or walnut milk) 3/4 cup to one cup depending if you like smoothie thick or more watery.
- Ice -1/4 cup.
- Blueberries- handful.
- 1/4 cup apple juice.

It's a healthy, gluten-free, dairy-free diet and provides energy. This diet also keeps my skin clear (no breakouts). If I eat eggs or oats, then I breakout. And I can't have milk or gluten. If I do, I must raise my medicine significantly. Maybe this will help any of you battling autoimmune conditions.

I also sleep with EMF blankets (one under me and one on top with a scarf one on my head). My blankets are actually baby blankets called "Shield Your Body." I have one for Eden too. I even at times will wear them around the house like an apron. One is bright pink with polka dots and the other blue with polka dots. I have a belt that I can hold them up with.

It's really silly looking. Once, I forgot I was wearing them when I walked outside to say goodbye to my mom, and the neighbor was just staring at me. My mom and I laughed so hard. I think she forgot what I was wearing too, but I won't be surprised if the neighbor never says hi to me ever again. I turn my Wi-Fi router off every night as well and put the phone on airplane mode and keep it away from my head. I do the same for Emilio and have taught my parents do it at their house. Ever since implementing this, I dream every night and have better energy. Studies show if you dream nightly, you are getting deep REM sleep, which helps to heal the body. All of these things are second nature to me, and I can do then without any real thought given to it, but at first it took some getting used to.

Lord, if any of these tips can help my readers, please bless their efforts to honor you with their bodies in this fallen world. We also recognize that you can sustain us even if we don't do any of these things.

Joni Eareckson-Tada recently said that she can't believe her old quadriplegic body is still going. She has outlived anyone with her condition. And Lord, you can and will sustain us until we finish the race. Help my readers to do whatever they need to to finish the one that you have marked out for them. Amen.

"Therefore I urge you, brethren, by the mercies of God, to present your bodies a living and holy sacrifice, acceptable to God, which is your spiritual service of worship."

Romans 12:1

⚘ REPLENISH ⚘

*"So then, while we have opportunity, let us do good to all
people, and especially to those who are of the household of the
faith."*

⚘Galatians 6:10

*A*ugust 18, 2019

Eden asked me yesterday if the serpents on the Ark were
nice? I thought that was a good question. I said, "We will just
have to ask Noah in Heaven." Of course, I imagine they were.
As if to say God tamed them to get in the Ark, and then Noah
caged them. I posted on Facebook a video of Eden asking the
question, and someone commented, "This touched my heart.
Your PRECIOUS child obviously takes GOD'S WORD quite
seriously and knows the story of Adam and Eve. She is correlat-
ing that to this image, and it is a highly observant and excellent
question. May we all have the same humble curiosity as we seek
the TRUTH and WISDOM from our LORD and SAVIOR
JESUS CHRIST. Thank you for sharing, it is a blessing!"

Something struck me tonight. I was the only grandchild to
both sets of my grandparents. Eden is my parent's only grandchild, and I want that to end with either me or Eden (whoever
has a child first). Meaning either I would have another child
(by God's grace which seems nearly impossible) or Eden will
have many and the one grandchild thing will end. That would
be great. Especially because God says, "Be fruitful and multiply" (Genesis 9:1).

Lord, I pray that you could bless our family with many
babies. I prayed for You to add babies to our church, and now

our church is exploding with babies. We have four new infants and three ladies expecting. Please continue to add to that number! It is so wonderful to see, truly.

Sometimes when we are struggling with things we can feel as if we aren't bearing any fruit or God is not using us, but just like a seed when it has been planted you cannot see what is going on under the soil, but something is happening, and in time it will show. We must stay faithful and not grow weary in doing good because God promises we will reap a harvest (Galatians 6:9).

"So then, while we have opportunity, let us do good to all people, and especially to those who are of the household of the faith."

⇒Galatians 6:10

⤙ SHINE ⤚

> *"The judgments of the LORD are true, they are righteous altogether. They are more desirable than gold, yes, than much fine gold; Sweeter also than honey and the drippings of the honeycomb."*
>
> ⤏Psalms 19:9b-10

*A*ugust 19, 2019

Today at church, Eden had a bit of sad face, and of course, it makes me sad to see that. I don't know why she was looking that way, but during worship it lifted. I was reminded that when she seems downcast, I feel as if it reflects on me as a parent. Even though it may be nothing I did, it still makes me feel as if she is just not happy overall, and that affects me. And perhaps the same is true for us when our eyes are dim or our faces sour, it reflects on our Maker. As if to say we are not content or happy with our lot. May our faces shine for Him so that we reflect that we are delighted in Him and glad to be His. Of course, all of this must be balanced with Ecclesiastes 3:4, which says there is a time "to weep and a time to laugh, a time to mourn and a time to dance."

God knows we will not be happy all the time and that many times our face will be the dead give away. That is why He placed so many medicinal remedies in His Word for His weary children. May these few touch you as they did me.

> *Psalm 31:16, 'Make Your face shine on Your servant; save me by Your loving devotion."*
>
> *Psalm 67:1, "May God be gracious to us and bless us, and cause His face to shine upon us."*

Psalm 80:3, "Restore us, O God, and cause Your face to shine upon us, that we may be saved."

Psalm 42:5, "Why are you downcast, O my soul? Why the unease within me? Put your hope in God, for I shall yet praise Him for the salvation of His presence.

Psalm 43:5, "Why are you downcast, O my soul? Why the unease within me? Put your hope in God, for I shall yet praise Him, my Savior, and my God."

Psalm 119:135, "Make Your face shine upon Your servant, and teach me Your statutes."

Proverbs 15:13. "A joyful heart makes a cheerful countenance, but sorrow of the heart crushes the spirit."

Proverbs 12:25, "Anxiety in a man's heart weighs it down, but a good word makes it glad."

Isaiah 50:4. "The Lord GOD has given Me the tongue of discipleship, to sustain the weary with a word. He awakens Me morning by morning; He awakens My ear to listen as a disciple."

We try to go to a restaurant called Hat Creek every Sunday after church. Eden typically takes a nap in the car, and then we go in and order our food. It's a great time, mainly because they have a play area that is huge and well kept. Eden loves to grab my hand and run fast while my mom chases us. The young worker there saw us getting out of our car as he was taking trash to the dumpster and yelled, "Hi Eden!" When the workers know your child by name you know you are there too often. Ha.

Tonight as we ran around the play area, I was reminded how wonderful it is that Eden trusts me to hold her hand while she runs knowing I will watch to make sure she doesn't run into anything. She is so focused on what is right in front of her that she can't see what could be around the corner. But I can. I'm bigger and can scan the whole play yard to make sure there is no danger ahead. And she can rest (run) assured that she is in good hands, no pun intended. The same is true of the Lord. He can see what is around the bend for us. He knows what is coming up, and we must hold his hand to get us through it. He knows how to guide us better than we know how to guide ourselves. Psalm 32:8 says that He will "guide us with his eye."

Yesterday we finished painting the schoolroom. It's a beautiful light purple color. Right now, the room is empty, so it's a lot of fun to play in and plan for how to set it up. I opened up the closet to find a lot of Eden's toys that she hadn't seen in a long time. Memory is a powerful thing because she pulled out two little stuffed animals and said, "Aw...you bought this little dog for me when I was sick, and Meesie bought me this rabbit." I was shocked because I bought her the dog over a year ago last Christmas when she turned 2 years old. May we use our powerful memories to recall His Word, which is more precious than hidden treasure.

"The judgments of the LORD are true, they are righteous altogether. They are more desirable than gold, yes, than much fine gold; Sweeter also than honey and the drippings of the honeycomb."

Psalms 19:9b-10

⋙ GENTLE ⋘

"Be anxious for nothing, but in everything by prayer and supplication with thanksgiving let your requests be made known to God."

Philippians 4:6

*A*ugust 20, 2019

I think I lost half my hair tonight. Before bed, Eden had a wild hair (pun intended) and wanted to do my hair with all her "soaps" that she made out of her new crayons. The blue crayon was a blueberry scent, red was raspberry, and so forth. She wanted to go through every crayon and put it on my hair as pretend soap. She would ask me over and over, "Which flavor do you prefer?" It was so dear. She would "wash" my hair and then let it dry. During the washing part, I could feel the pulls on my scalp, but she was having so much fun, and so was I, that I didn't dare say a word until I saw a pile of hair on the floor. She was much more tender after I explained how to wash gently or no one will want to go to her for a hairdo. And she moved right on to the next flavor to apply to my hair. I like how well she received the instruction. With zero questions. She just said, "Oh, okay." And made the change.

Wouldn't it be great if we could receive correction from the Lord that way? That, after hearing a sermon that instructs us in a new way or when we are corrected when reading His Word, we simply say, "Oh, okay."

Lord, help our hearts to be pliable to your words to receive correction and not be like the man in the book of James who hears the Word and then forgets it. We desire to be doers of the Word and not just hearers, lest we deceive ourselves.

I prayed last night that God would resurrect Eden's desire to look at my jewelry. I loved when she was little how she would look at every piece with excitement. I even got online to look for a jewelry box to buy for her. I never did, but I submitted my desire to the Lord. Then tonight, I could not believe my ears when after brushing her teeth she said, "Mama, may I look at your jewelry?" I had not heard those words in a long time. Many times when a desire that is good crosses our minds it can be of the Lord. So instead of just "wishing" it would happen, why not take it to the Lord in prayer. Because wishing won't get you anywhere.

"Be anxious for nothing, but in everything by prayer and supplication with thanksgiving let your requests be made known to God."

Philippians 4:6

☙ DELIVERER ☙

"Whatever your hand finds to do, do it with all your might…"

Ecclesiastes 9:10

August 21, 2019

It's interesting that, in the Bible, God's people typically find themselves in trouble, and then He sends a deliverer if you would. People like Samson, Moses, Abraham, Elijah, Debra, Gideon, and the list goes on and on. All of those leaders fall short though and point us to the true Deliverer that will not let us down, and His name is Jesus. In fact, every person in the world will let us down in some way, shape or form, but not Him.

Tonight I was meditating on all of that plus thinking about the fact that it is hard for me to see my mom drive down the street to go home. It would be nice if we could all live together and she could do laundry at our house, and we could all share the same things and live in harmony. I could make her all her meals and do most the shopping. Like she did for me all my life growing up. But maybe God has not designed it that way for a reason. Perhaps God designed it differently so that we will enjoy heaven more. Because in heaven, we will all be in the same house with different "rooms." Jesus said in my Father's house are many mansions (rooms), and that He "goes to prepare a place for us" (John 14:2). It's wonderful to think about.

We decided to do a little bit of late-night painting outside before bed. It was Eden's idea. She asked, and I said, "Well, you have to take put something else on so that you don't get wet and full of paint." She quickly agreed, and we went outside, which was very warm. She was painting away when she got to the black paint and said, "This is like the pit." Then she got to the blue paint, she said, "This will be like heaven! Beautiful like heaven." To which I said, "Amen!"

I can't hardly get over the fact that tonight, for the first time in over two years, I don't have to hang up the black table cloths that I bought at the Dollar Store to keep the morning sun out. I've been hanging them up every night for about two years, and today the drapes my Aunt Vicki bought for us arrived. They are just for one room, but the installer took three hours to hang them. I had never had such fine treatment for a drape installation, but that's because I have never had drapes installed before. And then I learned there is a difference from a curtain and a drape. Who would have known?! The installer played lovely classical music the whole time too.

It made me think of the passage in the Old Testament in Exodus 35 where Moses calls out Bezalel and Oholiab and God uses the two men skillfully for His glory to tend to the tabernacle with their craftmanship. The five verses in my mind were this:

> *30 Then Moses said to the sons of Israel, "See, the LORD has called by name Bezalel the son of Uri, the son of Hur, of the tribe of Judah. 31 And He has filled him with the Spirit of God, in wisdom, in understanding and in knowledge and in all craftsmanship; 32 to make designs for working in gold and in silver and in bronze, 33 and in the cutting of stones for settings and in the carving of wood, so as to perform in every inventive work. 34 He also has put in his heart to teach, both he and Oholiab, the son of Ahisamach, of the tribe of Dan. 35 He has filled them with skill to perform every work of an engraver and of a designer and of an embroiderer, in blue and in purple and in scarlet material, and in fine linen, and of a weaver, as performers of every work and makers of designs.*

I could just imagine Bezalel and Oholiab must have had so much delight in working on the tabernacle. Sort of like the man installing the drapes. He really seemed to be enjoying himself and was so peaceful about it. Like God created him to do the very thing he was delighting in. Maybe even Bezalel and Oholiab requested that worship music fill the tabernacle while they worked. In heaven, we can ask them if they did.

I certainly felt unworthy of the treatment and care this man was taking on our wall. I'm sure heaven will be like that. We will learn all the details of the Bible and true distinctions of words we've read and heard, and deep meanings that we have no clue about and feel unworthy of all the treatment we receive there. It will be like delightful music to our ears. I must say the curtains are so long that it makes us look very small and the ceiling very tall. Our whole perspective changed. I honestly didn't know our ceiling was so high. The way we had our blinds set up before didn't show the true scale of the room. The height of our ceiling did not change one bit, but our perspective did once a little time, and care and attention were given to just one wall. I know that when we give time and attention and care to our souls by ingesting the Word of God (just even mulling over one verse), results in new eyes and a new perspective of our surroundings. We begin to see lost people in places where perhaps we once did not. We begin tending and caring for our family members with love and diligence when as unbelievers we did not. Our local church will be a priority too, and we will seek to bless others more than ourselves (ouch).

Eden looked like a grasshopper tonight against the drapes as I read to her before bed. Maybe when I look at these drapes (which remind me of something that would've been in the temple), I will be reminded that the veil was torn through Christ and God conquered our enemies on the cross. I would never have known drapes could take on so much meaning. Maybe we should pray Aunt Vicki does our whole house. I'll remind her of the verse "It's better to give than to receive." Ha!

"Whatever your hand finds to do, do it with all your might..."

Ecclesiastes 9:10

"For behold, I will create
new heavens and a new earth.
The former things will not be remembered,
nor will they come to mind.
But be glad and rejoice forever
in what I create;"

Isaiah 65:17-18

August 22, 2019

I was deeply ministered to by Isaiah 65:17-25. I looked up what Spurgeon had to say about that passage, and really liked what he said: "The resurrection will be to the body what regeneration is to the soul." Wow.

And Isaiah 65:19 is life-altering if we believe it. It's good news for those who often weep (and if you are a mom you will undoubtedly do that a lot). Like I did last night. I wept over the goodness of the Lord, over my lack of walking in the Spirit and wept wanting to seek God for fresh grace and renewed vision. Just before bed, I landed on Isaiah 65:19 where God is talking about the New Heavens and New Earth and says, "I will rejoice over Jerusalem and take delight in my people; the sound of weeping and of crying will be heard in it NO MORE." How wonderful! I will try to imagine it without weeping.

"For behold, I will create
new heavens and a new earth.
The former things will not be remembered,
nor will they come to mind.
But be glad and rejoice forever
in what I create;"

Isaiah 65:17-18

⌒ KINDNESS ⌒

"Be kind to one another, tender-hearted…"

Ephesians 4:32a

*A*ugust 23, 2019

I suddenly lost it laughing as Eden was "checking" me out at her grocery store with her cash register and scanner. It struck me funny how she managed to stuff everything, plus the kitchen sink, in this miniature-shopping cart she has. I was laughing so hard that I was crying, when just as suddenly I had great compassion for all of the people at grocery stores and places that check us out because they are someone's children. I thought if Eden ever worked at a store, I would want the customers to be so kind to her. I think one of the kindest things we can ever do for cashiers is to thank them and give them a gospel tract. Like today, I had to return two items at two different stores. It was terrific handing out tracts, and the young man at the UPS store said, "Yes, you've given this to me before." To which I said, "Great! It will be your reminder to watch Unpopular."

"Be kind to one another, tender-hearted..."

⇒Ephesians 4:32a

⇜ TEARLESS ⇝

"The voice of weeping shall be no more heard."

⇒Isaiah 65:19

*A*ugust 24, 2019

My friend Liz posted this great word from Charles Spurgeon on her Facebook page around the time I was writing the above post from yesterday's entry:

Morning and Evening by Charles Haddon Spurgeon

"The voice of weeping shall be no more heard." Isaiah 65:19 The glorified weep no more, for all outward causes of grief are gone. There are no broken friendships, nor blighted prospects in heaven. Poverty, famine, peril, persecution, and slander, are unknown there. No pain distresses, no thought of death or bereavement saddens. They weep no more, for they are perfectly sanctified. No "evil heart of unbelief" prompts them to depart from the living God; they are without fault before his throne, and are fully conformed to his image. Well may they cease to mourn who have ceased to sin. They weep no more, because all fear of change is past. They know that they are eternally secure. Sin is shut out, and they are shut in. They dwell within a city which shall never be stormed; they bask in a sun which shall never set; they drink of a river which shall never dry; they pluck fruit from a tree which shall never wither. Countless cycles may revolve, but eternity shall not be exhausted, and while eternity endures, their immortality and blessedness shall co-exist with it. They are forever with the Lord. They weep no more, because every desire is fulfilled. They cannot wish for anything which they have not in possession. Eye and ear, heart and hand, judgment, imagination, hope, desire, will, all the faculties, are completely satisfied; and imperfect as our present ideas are of the things which God hath prepared for them that love him, yet we know enough, by the revelation of the Spirit, that the saints above are supremely blessed. The joy of Christ, which is an infinite fullness of delight, is in them. They bathe themselves in the bottomless, shoreless sea of infinite beatitude. That same joyful rest remains for us. It may not be far distant. Ere long the weeping willow shall be exchanged for the palm-branch of victory, and sorrow's dewdrops will be transformed into the pearls of everlasting bliss. "Wherefore comfort one another with these words."

"The voice of weeping shall be no more heard."

Isaiah 65:19

⤍ LISTENING ⤏

August 25, 2019

Yesterday I started singing, "Power in the blood!" as I held Eden in my arms and swung her around the bathroom. She wanted to do it again and again, so I did. I rocked her and then spun around when the "power in the blood" part came up.

The song was still stuck in my head today while driving in the car to church. I sang it, and Eden hummed almost the whole way. When the PowerPoint came on for worship, I was quite surprised to see the same song! I went up to our worship leader after service and told him what had happened. He said, "This is only the second time I've ever played it for the church." Wow! He's been doing worship for our church for two years. What a nice reminder that God is mindful of his people and is listening to us (Psalm 139:4) and taking pleasure in it.

"For the LORD takes pleasure in His people…"

Psalm 149:4a

⋘ JOY ⋙

"Cast your burden upon the Lord, and He will sustain you; He will never let the righteous be shaken."

⟹Psalm 55:22

*A*ugust 26, 2019

Elisabeth Elliot (wisely) said, "Everything, if given to God, can become your gateway to joy."

"Cast your burden upon the Lord, and He will sustain you; He will never let the righteous be shaken."

⟹Psalm 55:22

∝ STORY ∝

August 30, 2019

I'm sure you have heard of writer's block. It's when writers hit a wall and can't think of anything to write about. I have had that for a bit with writing songs to help us memorize scripture. So I prayed about it and was thankful today to come up with three new songs for creation days four, five, and six in Genesis 1. I will be amazed if we can memorize all of chapter 1. May Eden always remember what we've sung so far for all her days.

I've also started telling her an imaginary story called "The Glory Garden," which I modeled after the Narnia series. There are animal characters that all have issues with sin until they happen upon a rather unusual place called "The Glory Garden." She begs me to tell her Frog's story again or Llama's story or Panda's or Bat's. If you are reading this, please pray that God would give me the time and energy to turn it into a book.

Today Eden pretended to call "the Lord Jesus on the phone" so she could ask Him what day He created all the flowers. She wanted to know, "Was it on day 3 or day 4?"

P.S. I have never tried to call the Lord on the phone. Ha.

❧ WORK ❧

"And there will no longer be any night; and they will not have need of the light of a lamp nor the light of the sun, because the Lord God will illumine them; and they will reign forever and ever"

Revelation 22:5

*A*ugust 31, 2019

If I'm left to myself long enough, I tend to become overwhelmed by a ton of cares. Mostly the concerns are about Eden and her future and what I desire for her. Presently I'm trying to teach her as much scripture as I can through songs. For a while there I had a bit of a writing block. But since God's Word says to "sing to Him a new song," (Psalm 33:3) I prayed for new songs and yesterday had a good day of writing a few. Today I sang the new song a few times and played on the guitar and felt the words sink in a bit regarding day 4 of Genesis 1. The Lord was very busy on that day; busy hanging the stars and the sun and the moon for us. He must value work and productivity a lot because even though He could have brought everything into existence by the snap of his finger, He instead worked for six days straight and then rested as a show of His sovereignty. It reminds me of a lady I met once who saw our service dog Lilly and said, "I'm glad you are working her and that you made her a working dog because she will live longer that way." She added, "We once had a dog similar to yours, and she lived to be very old because we didn't just let her lay around." Her words have stuck with me. Since Eden came into our lives, Lilly has not worked as much, however. She still receives her nightly walk and is treated with exceptional care, but I noticed that if she doesn't work much then she doesn't have much of an appetite. The same is true for us humans as well, and hunger is the best sauce.

The Lord certainly had man's hunger in mind when he created all kinds of food on day 3 of creation. God knew man was going to tend the garden pre-fall. He knew he would require food and feel hunger (I imagine there was hunger before the fall) and that God would satisfy Adam and Eve with good things like food (Psalm 145:16). So he gives man hunger and then gives him the source (food) to satisfy him. Just like us He gives us a hunger for Him and then He gives us Himself to satisfy us.

It's interesting to me that if I look back over my life I find that God puts burdens or desires on my heart for certain things and then I go to Him in prayer (which of course is wrought of Him) and He answers with the desire being fulfilled or removes the desire or changes me in some way to align with His will. A current desire of mine is to one-day help Eden own her own little business or work for herself (perhaps walking dogs) or something like that. She likes to clean and be busy cleaning. I went to my mom's house tonight, and Eden cleaned her already spotless sink for 15 minutes. It was so sweet. Maybe she will clean homes and run her own business that way. Or perhaps she can help assist me in real estate. I just don't know. I pray she will use her hands for God's glory.

I desire that she marry someone who can take care of her and be able to provide so she can stay home with children and enjoy herself and clean her own home. I fear that there are not many people raising their children like we are raising Eden and it seems impossible that there be a suitor for her that we would love, but I know God has His remnant and He will remember Eden (Psalm 100:5).

So, tonight Lord, I cast my care about Eden's future on you. I pray for all my readers as well, and their cares and concerns for their children. Your Word says to "cast your cares on the Lord, and He will sustain you" (Psalm 55:22). What a comforting verse. You want us to give our cares to you, and in return, You will sustain us. What a trade-off. I feel better just unloading everything onto You. Thank you Lord for listening and Good night, Lord. Oh, and it's funny to think that in Heaven I will never again say good "night" as there will be no more night. Amen!

"And there will no longer be any night; and they will not have need of the light of a lamp nor the light of the sun, because the Lord God will illumine them; and they will reign forever and ever"

Revelation 22:5

⤙ FOLLOW ⤚

"Father, I desire that they also, whom You have given Me, be with Me where I am, so that they may see My glory which You have given Me, for You loved Me before the foundation of the world."

⇒John 17:24

September 1, 2019

Before bed, Eden wanted to put little Minnie Mouse next to her big Minnie Mouse because "she wants to sleep next to her Mama." This just melted my heart. She had me wrap little Minnie up and then I left her to situate them. After Eden was fast asleep, I saw that she had them facing each other.

My mom loves to follow me around. She always has. And I know why now that I'm a mom and I've told her many times (even recently and I'm 42) "it's okay for you to follow me at church or stand next to me. I don't mind at all." And I hope Eden doesn't mind me doing the same to her one day. I tend to follow her in the house a lot, but she follows me more and tells me, "I will go where you go." I pray that will be a continual true statement.

Something struck me tonight as I was reading Matthew 28:20. Jesus is saying a farewell to his disciples, and in so many words, He says to each one personally, "I will be where you are." It's as if He is saying, "I will follow you." Or "I'll go where you go." In fact, He says, "Lo, I am with you always, even to the end of the age." The important part is that the "you" here is not a plural you. Meaning he is talking to the individual. He could have said I will be with "you all" or, in California terms, "you guys", but he chose to say YOU. I'll be with YOU. I will always be with YOU.

The word "you" is υμων (hymōn) in the Greek. It's a personal/possessive pronoun meaning you or thou. If we are His sheep, this is deeply comforting. He is with us in trials, in pain, in sorrow, in joy, in laughter, in significant life changes, in life and in death, in every season. No wonder moms and dads love to follow their children around. Like when their children move to another state, typically they do too. They want to be with them (this is a godly desire and longing). God plants that desire in the heart because He too is with His children. He desires to be with us (John 17:24) and is with us (Matthew 28:20) I'm so glad my mom moved from California to live just seven minutes away from us. What a blessing.

"Father, I desire that they also, whom You have given Me, be with Me where I am, so that they may see My glory which You have given Me, for You loved Me before the foundation of the world."

☙John 17:24

∼ CAST ∼

"Casting all your anxieties on him, because he cares for you."

⇒1 Peter 5:7

*S*eptember 2, 2019

I pray a lot for whomever it is Eden will marry. That he will be humble man and have no guile, and love her and treat her well and that he will fear the Lord and be peaceable, and a good listener and then I realized I was describing the Lord and no one can possibly measure up to Him. Still I pray and trust and wait and see how He answers knowing that He hears and He desires that I cast all my cares on him because He cares for me (1 Peter 5:6-7). That goes for you too, dear reader. What is your care tonight? What is it that seems to always be on the back burner cooking in your mind? Is it your children's salvation? Cast it to the Lord. Is it your failure as a parent? Cast it to the Lord. Is it worry about the salvation of other family members? Cast it to the Lord. Is it wondering how you will make the next month's ends meet? Cast it to the Lord. Is your failing health ailing you? Cast it to the Lord. Is it that you would like to spend more time with your children that are grown? Cast it to the Lord. Is it that your sinful past stole many of your prime years? Cast it to the Lord.

Isn't it great that in every season and every situation we can cast things to the Lord? Imagine what a fisherman does when he casts his line into the water. He has to give his pole a good thrust and then hope that the line will go down in just the right spot so that a fish will see the bait and take a bite. When we thrust our cares to God, we don't have to wonder if He will see it or hear it, we have His word that He will (1

Peter 3:12). We are not like a fisherman just hoping the line will reach the right spot. Our line (if you would) goes directly to the source it needs to, which is right to God's ear. Our job then is to be patient on His answer; not to become restless. Just like the fisherman. When they cast their line into the water, sometimes the waiting for a tug can seem like an eternity. But the patient fisherman will get a reward with diligence and persistence. So too must we be this way in prayer. Be diligent and persistent.

"Casting all your anxieties on him, because he cares for you."

1 Peter 5:7

TURNING

"You have turned for me my mourning into dancing; You have loosed my sackcloth and girded me with gladness."

=Psalm 30:11

*S*eptember 3, 2019

I was teaching Eden about Jesus' first miracle of turning water into wine and how the Lord is in the business of turning things. And I don't mean turning things like turning doorknobs. And she laughed. But what I do mean is turning things around. Like situations. Like turning our mourning into dancing, and I asked her what mourning was, and she made a crying sound. He also likes to turn around situations like storms. He can take a terrible storm and make it peaceful. He also is in the business of turning hearts around and making them soft. What a mighty God we serve!

"You have turned for me my mourning into dancing; You have loosed my sackcloth and girded me with gladness."

=Psalm 30:11

↪ VALUABLE ↩

*S*eptember 4, 2019

Eden said right before bed that she was so excited for the baby. She was referring to the bird's nest we found in our tree. We spent about an hour outside tonight sitting and talking about what the birds were doing as a big flock flew over. They were so loud we could hear them cackling three houses down. Then I found a nest in our tree. I told Eden that the birds were scrambling to make everything perfect for the new baby bird and how they were "fluffing the pillows" and "making the food". She wanted me to tell her the story over and over. She inched herself closer and closer and hung on every word. Many hours later, I had forgotten all about it, but she had not and said, "I'm so excited about the new baby." I'll have to ask her if she thinks the birds were busy storing up food in a barn for the baby. Then I'll tell her these verses in Matthew 6:26-27 *"Look at the birds of the air, for they neither sow nor reap nor gather into barns; yet your heavenly Father feeds them. Are you not of more value than they? Which of you by worrying can add one cubit to his stature?"*

"You have filled my heart with more joy than when grain and new wine abound."

⟠Psalm 4:7

⤞ FRUITFUL ⤝

*"And now it has pleased You to bless the house of Your servant,
that it may continue forever before You; for You, O LORD,
have blessed, and it is blessed forever"*

—1 Chronicles 17:27

*S*eptember 5, 2019

I got a book from the library about a baby's first year of life. It has adorable pictures, but as soon as Eden saw the cover she said, "Hmmm...I don't like this."

"Hmmm....I wonder why?" I said.

"Well...'cubz it's ugly."

I have never heard her utter the word ugly, nor do I make a practice of saying it, so it was a shock to hear her say such a thing. Maybe one of the children's books had the word in it. I racked my brain to think where she got it from. She has also done things such as turning books over that have babies on the cover and commenting about not liking her twin baby dolls. I was encouraged last night however when my mom and I asked Eden if she wanted to be a doctor or a teacher or a dentist or a dog trainer and she said no until we asked if she wanted to be a mom to which she said yes. My heart leapt for joy at hearing that, so today I prayed over her as she napped that God would make her womb fruitful, for both her joy and her husband's (and mine and Emilio's of course). I know of several ladies that have many children, one friend having nine the last I counted and she seems to have a permanent smile on her face. I pray that will be true of Eden one day.

Another encouragement from yesterday was that Eden "read" to me almost an entire children's book on John Newton's life. She memorized it after having it read to her several times. John Newton wrote Amazing Grace, one of the most famous hymns in history.

Amazing grace, how sweet the sound,

that saved a wretch like me.

I once was lost, but now am found,

Was blind but now I see.

In fact, he composed the song on the very boat that God saved him on.

Did I mention Newton was an only child just like Eden? This certainly serves to remind us that, whether nine children or one, all wombs are fruitful.

"And now it has pleased You to bless the house of Your servant, that it may continue forever before You; for You, O LORD, have blessed, and it is blessed forever"

1 Chronicles 17:27

❧ DISCIPLINE ❧

"Therefore be imitators of God as dear children."

≋Ephesians 5:1

*S*eptember 6, 2019

Lately, I feel as if I've lost a lot of ground with disciplining. When my thyroid acts up, I slow down, and so does the world around me. It took everything within me to clean the house today. I started in my room by neatly making the bed and clearing out anything that didn't belong. That helped me to feel like I accomplished something. Then I cleaned another room, and Eden said, "May I help you?" So she helped and went everywhere I went, which I loved. Then I moved to our front entryway, which was a mess. I had things in there from a project I was working on that needed moving to its proper place. Then came the dreaded kitchen.

It took 45 minutes to muscle my way through cleaning every dish, wiping the counters, and cleaning the floor. I felt better afterward, though, like I could think better. I think my energy is low because I have not been eating well. When I deviate and eat any dairy, it clogs the liver pathways which prevents the medicine from absorbing well and then I need to up the medicine. I also threw my neck out last week while putting on my dress for church, and it still hurts. Go ahead and laugh. I'm laughing as I write.

I also feel like there is so little time. I want to stop the clock and teach Eden more and more of the Bible. I can only do so much in a day, and my spirit is so willing, but there are days it's hard to get this body in gear. When others come over, and they are full of life, it can be hard for me to match it. I know God doesn't call me to do that, but still, I try my best.

I also want to aim to not allow playtime during our family devotions, as those times are so important, and I feel like I've lost ground there. We have not been as consistent as I would like. There really is no excuse for it.

Tonight, for example, we skipped devotion, but my parents were over for their 28th-anniversary celebration. We prayed for a while together, during which Eden quietly came over to me and whispered, "Can I do your hair?" How could I turn her down? It was so sweet. We, of course, prayed for her salvation, asking God to save her as early as possible. My mom shared with me that she met a young man at In-N-Out just yesterday, who told her that he became a Christian at age four. My mom was deeply encouraged by that, as he seemed genuinely saved.

Later on, I happened upon a testimony of a friend of Elizabeth Elliot, named Katharine Howard, whose daughter was saved young. She said, "My younger daughter recalls when at the age of 4 she and I knelt by my bed and she asked the Lord Jesus to come into her heart. She says that she never doubted her salvation since then." She goes on to say, "Remember the loving invitation of the Lord, '*Suffer the little children to come unto Me and forbid them not, for such us he kingdom of heaven*' (Matthew 19:14).'" She closed her thought by saying, "God grant that none of our little ones will have to say later in life the sad words from Proverbs 5:12-14, *"You will say, 'How I hated discipline! How my heart spurned correction! I would not obey my teachers or turn my ear to my instructors. And I was soon in serious trouble in the assembly of God's people."* Help this not be our children, Lord. And what matters the end of the day is not what great parents we are but rather what a great God You are. Amen.

"Therefore be imitators of God as dear children."

Ephesians 5:1

∽ CONTENTMENT ∽

"This book of the law shall not depart from your mouth, but you shall meditate on it day and night, so that you may be careful to do according to all that is written in it; for then you will make your way prosperous, and then you will have success."

Joshua 1:8

*S*eptember 7, 2019

Having Eden in our home is like a dream. She has so much life, and every day is fun. I don't want to wake up from it. I went to Sprouts today and saw a little girl that was about one year younger than Eden. I couldn't stop staring at her and thinking about how she looked like Eden. Her hair and everything. And then my heart got sad at how fast time has gone. How quickly I can break the 10th commandment and covet if I'm not on guard.

It's funny how the scripture says not to covet your neighbor's oxen or wife, and perhaps child should be added to the list. Godliness with contentment is great gain, indeed (1 Timothy 6:6).

Then for just a minute, I was on Facebook scrolling through my newsfeed and happened upon a lady having her fifth baby. And my mind wanted to get sad again. Now I know why John Calvin said, "Our hearts are idol factories." If we are not careful, we can pump out new idols every hour. We must keep a watch and a guard on our hearts for out of it flows the issues of life (Proverbs 4:23). I had a friend tell me she got off Facebook and social media for a week, and it changed her mood. She was more happy and content. I bet! No wonder Facebook is so successful; it sucks us in like a trap and then it's hard to get out.

Lord, teach us to balance things that are good but can turn rancid. Like going to the store (that's a good thing) and Facebook (can be used for good). Help us to use all things for Your glory, and when we struggle and battle with covetousness and wanting more or different than our current lot, help us to repent and receive your grace. Amen.

Before bed, Eden was thumbing (literally) through her children's bible. I could hardly handle the sight. Her thumb is so small, and I don't know how such a little thing has such precision. It's adorable to watch. And I think she delighted in me delighting in her doing it. So she kept thumbing through the pages until she landed on three crosses. She stopped to gaze at the picture. I wasn't sure what she was thinking, but finally she compassionately said, "Awe," and asked if it was the Lord "on there". And she wondered who the other two people were next to Him? I told her they were sinners and thieves, but Jesus was not but he was treated like he was one for us. It was a special way to end the day.

Later I thought, I bet the Lord smiles as He watches us read through His word. Age doesn't matter either. Young or old, it's sweet to see someone carefully comb through the pages of the bible. I hope this week, we endeavor to comb through our Bibles a bit more, and think of God delighting in us as we do. It brings me joy when I know someone is taking the time to read one of my books. It is a blessing that anyone would give of their time and energy to it. I'm sure I inherited such thoughts from Him.

"This book of the law shall not depart from your mouth, but you shall meditate on it day and night, so that you may be careful to do according to all that is written in it; for then you will make your way prosperous, and then you will have success."

≈Joshua 1:8

*"In the fear of the LORD there is strong confidence,
And his children will have refuge."*

⟹Proverbs 14:26

*S*eptember 12, 2019

I received a heartbreaking email from a dear lady that I met a decade ago at the Deeper Conference that I was working at with Kirk Cameron and Ray Comfort.

She wrote:

"Hey Trish, you are doing such an amazing job with Eden! I love how she sings and has memorized Scripture. I could really use tips and advice on how to raise my little girl right, to pour God's word into her. I don't know where or how to start. I've had a rough go the past couple of years (ever) since my husband walked out on our marriage. I'm still waist-high in a lengthy legal battle to deal with this separation/divorce, so I haven't had the chance to stop and breathe and figure out how to parent to help my little girl to know Christ. I still haven't been able to process what my husband did emotionally, but life doesn't stand still, and your kids won't pause growing up until you've recovered from life events. I'm always lost in between the legal battle and trying to make sure I can put food on the table when I never thought I'd be in this position of single-mom-hood. But especially lately, I've thought more and more about my little girl's spiritual well being. I don't know how or where to start to begin actively teaching my daughter about God and teaching her the word, and how to make it doable for a 3yr old to absorb and understand and follow. Can you tell me what sorts of things you're doing with Eden on a daily or weekly basis? What resources or materials do you use with Eden? What specific CDs/music do you play around the house for Eden to listen to? Are there books that are age-appropriate for Eden's age that you find is helping her to memorize Scripture or biblical concepts? Etc."

This was my reply via four short voice clips, so excuse the poor grammar:

"Thank you so much for writing to me. It pains me to read about your current situation. I'm going to pray that God will give you the strength to sail your boat in the storm. It's very easy to sail a boat when the waves are calm, but when the storm is raging, that is when we really get to put into practice our sailing skills. That is when God will plant our roots deep and cause us to grow.

I pray for you that during the storm, God will cause you to grow deeply, and your roots will sink deep into Him. I also am praying Romans 8:28 for you that God will work everything out for good, even this terrible situation.

I want to encourage you not to overwhelm yourself with too many things. Just play "Seeds Family Worship" songs or some worship throughout the day and then sing, sing, sing! That is what Eden and I do, and that is how we are memorizing a lot of Scripture.

And then grab yourself a copy of The Beginner's Bible and read it, especially before bed at night. It takes Eden and me about one month to go through the entire book, cover to cover. We've done this twice. I'm praying for you."

Later that evening, Eden and I decided to get our money together for the Lord so that she could drop it in the offering box at church at church on Sunday. We put a lot of offering envelopes together at once so that I always have them in my purse.

We simply place one-dollar bills into each envelope and write "Offering to God from Eden" on the front. Eden will typically put a cute sticker on too. She loves putting the money inside and sealing the envelope. Today she said, "Mama, I love the church." And I must say that I love that she said that!

"In the fear of the LORD there is strong confidence,
And his children will have refuge."

⸗Proverbs 14:26

⋘ HABITS ⋙

"For the LORD gives wisdom;
From His mouth come knowledge and understanding."

═Proverbs 2:6

*S*eptember 13, 2019

I stayed up late last night listening to a message by Joel Beeke. It was fantastic. It was 70 minutes of him teaching on parenting. He said many things that were worth putting in this book. Here's a few I jotted down:

"We need holy habits in our lives, and family worship is one of them." He said that if he missed a day of family worship, his children would look at him and say, "Is everything OK with you?" This can be a rather convicting statement as we can tend to have all sorts of other habits, but then neglect to have family worship.

He also said, "We will either be the best or worst book our children will ever read." He was speaking of the example we set, then went on to say that as parents, "we are to be our children's mentors."

Beeke also mentioned that his father was very godly and would not miss family worship time for the world. He would often tell the children, "we can't miss any of you in heaven." And what he meant by not "missing" them in heaven was that he wanted them in heaven. That like a piece in a puzzle is missing, he didn't want them to be missing from heaven, if you would. And Praise God, all the children were saved. I thought that was sweet.

Every morning when we wake up, I try to pray with Eden. We also pick out scripture to read for the day and sing a song. Today I decided to ask Eden what her prayer request was. Immediately, she started to pray, "Dear Lord, I pray for big Mickey Mouse and big Minnie Mouse at Disneyland that they will read the tract and get saved." She was so sincere about that prayer as I have told her that there are real people in those costumes, so maybe she understands.

During our rest time, I was reading to her and talking about Noah's Ark. I asked her, "How many doors were there on the Ark?" She held up one finger and kept it up.

I then asked her, "How many ways are there to heaven?" She again held up one finger and kept it up." I explained to her that just like people needed to enter into the Ark through the one door to be saved from the rain, we need to enter through the one door of Jesus Christ to be saved from God's judgment.

It's a lot for a two-year-old to grasp such an analogy, but I look forward to and pray for the day she does.

"For the LORD gives wisdom;
From His mouth come knowledge and understanding."

⁼Proverbs 2:6

❧ ENCOURAGEMENT ❧

"Indeed, the LORD will comfort Zion; He will comfort all her waste places. And her wilderness He will make like Eden, And her desert like the garden of the LORD; Joy and gladness will be found in her. Thanksgiving and sound of a melody."

⟞Isaiah 51:3

*S*eptember 14, 2019

Just read these verses from Isaiah 35:3-10. What an encouragement!

3 Encourage the exhausted, and strengthen the feeble.

4 Say to those with anxious heart, "Take courage, fear not. Behold, your God will come with vengeance; The recompense of God will come, But He will save you."

5 Then the eyes of the blind will be opened And the ears of the deaf will be unstopped.

6 Then the lame will leap like a deer, And the tongue of the mute will shout for joy. For waters will break forth in the wilderness And streams in the Arabah.

7 The scorched land will become a pool And the thirsty ground springs of water; In the haunt of jackals, its resting place, Grass becomes reeds and rushes.

8 A highway will be there, a roadway, And it will be called the Highway of Holiness. The unclean will not travel on it, But it will be for him who walks that way, And fools will not wander on it.

9 No lion will be there, Nor will any vicious beast go up on it; These will not be found there. But the redeemed will walk there,

10 And the ransomed of the LORD will return And come with joyful shouting to Zion, With everlasting joy upon their heads. They will find gladness and joy, And sorrow and sighing will flee away.

"Indeed, the LORD will comfort Zion; He will comfort all her waste places. And her wilderness He will make like Eden, And her desert like the garden of the LORD; Joy and gladness will be found in her. Thanksgiving and sound of a melody."

⇒Isaiah 51:3

ᴏᴄ CLEANSING ᴄᴏ

"Then one of the seraphim flew to me with a burning coal in his hand, which he had taken from the altar with tongs. He touched my mouth with it and said, "Behold, this has touched your lips; and your iniquity is taken away and your sin is forgiven."

—Isaiah 6:6-7

*S*eptember 15, 2019

In a post a few days ago, I wrote a quote by Joel Beeke, where he says, "We will either be the best or worst book our children read." Ouch. That can be so true. And of course, as moms, we want never to lead our children astray. But that quote can be taken wrong. We can incorrectly take it to mean that we must live a fairytale life of never sinning and portraying that all is dandy, ensuring we leave our children with only wonderful memories of us. I must admit I like the way that sounds, but we must remember we are not in our perfected bodies yet. And we are not Christ.

I realize how elementary these truths are. However, if you are anything like me, you need the comforting reminder that we still have indwelling sin, just see 1 John 1:8 (which is not a license to sin of course). We will continue to battle sin here on earth (Eph 6:10). And, oh, what a battle it can be. Many times life catches us off guard. Sort of like it did Eve (1 Peter 5:8).

Eve was walking in the cool of the day, maybe even humming a tune, when she unexpectedly encountered the serpent and fell for the lie. Can you relate? Imagine you are walking along, enjoying your day. The children are peaceable; you feel good; when unexpectedly, they break out into crying or fits of anger or both. What do you do? You want to respond with patience, but you are so caught off guard by their behavior, that your anger is provoked, and before you know it, you've responded in a not so patient manner. After the 1-minute whirlwind passes, you regret your sinful response. Being the little sinners our children are, they don't see their sin as exceedingly sinful and quickly move on. Not us, though. We know what a stench sin is and can struggle with receiving God's grace rather than finding great comfort in it.

Our comfort when we stumble and fall is in the book we hope our children read and grow to love and live by...the Bible. It is filled with man's imperfections and sins and shortcomings and gives the only remedy for them. God uses sinful man to make the brilliance of Christ's holiness more magnified and glorious. God will use all our shortcomings for His glory and our good and we have His Word on it (Romans 8:28).

So when we think that we will never sin against our children or our spouse, think again and remember 1 John 1:9 is in the Bible because we need it (daily). I call that verse "The Christian's Bar of Soap" and use it for soul washing, for it says, "If we confess our sins, He is faithful and just to forgive us our sins and to cleanse us from all unrighteousness." What a comforting verse! He will cleanse us of all the sins not just some but all (ones we think are big and ones we think are small). He is faithful when we are not. He is righteous towards us when we are anything but that towards others. And He cleanses us, instantly restoring our communion with Him upon our confession. So, why are you still moping?

Remember the song, *Nothing But The Blood of Jesus*?

> *What can wash away my sin?*
> *Nothing but the blood of Jesus.*
> *What can make me whole again?*
> *Nothing but the blood of Jesus.*

Tonight on a walk with Eden, she saw two turtle lawn ornaments and asked if she could touch one. "Sure," I said.

"This one is the mama, and this one is the baby," she said.

Then she picked up the mama and said it was "heavy" in such a way that reminded me of the most adorably precious time she picked a piece of bark up off the ground and said, "This looks like the cross Jesus had, but it was much too heavy for Him to carry."

And yet carry it He did, along with our sorrows. (Isaiah 53:4).

I wanted to tell Eden, "You're right, that mama turtle is heavy, and so is my heart today." The only thing that could lift my spirit was thinking about Christ carrying the cross and bearing all my sin and sorrow. Yours too, dear reader, if you are in Christ and He in you. Sometimes our sins can be so terrible that we feel it too heavy to bear. And they are, but we are not supposed to bear them. We can't. Only God can.

So as I pushed Eden on her tricycle, I began singing *Power Of The Cross* by the Getty's:

> *That's the power of the cross*
> *Christ became sin for us*
> *Took the blame, bore the wrath*
> *We stand forgiven at the cross.*

As I sang, I saw Eden raising her little right arm as if to praise Him while she nodded her head. It was an extraordinary moment. I can see her arm in the sun and little hand raised in my mind's eye even as I type.

I heard once that "God lets people let us down so that we know HE is God and they are not." They will let us down and we will let them down. All designed by God so He get's glory and not us or them. May our hearts remember that when dealing with our little neighbors.

"Then one of the seraphim flew to me with a burning coal in his hand, which he had taken from the altar with tongs. He touched my mouth with it and said, "Behold, this has touched your lips; and your iniquity is taken away and your sin is forgiven."

⇐Isaiah 6:6-7

"Those who have insight will shine brightly like the brightness of the expanse of heaven, and those who lead the many to righteousness, like the stars forever and ever."

⟹Daniel 12:3

*S*eptember 16, 2019

We have a dear couple that attends our church along with their adorable little boy. Today, the husband said, "I like your book." It took me a minute to process what he said because even though my first book, *Struggles and Sunshine*, is written to encourage anyone and everyone, 99.9% of the feedback I've received has come from women.

So I said, "What....You're reading it??" He said, "Yes, I read it to my wife!" I was so surprised, and asked, "How did you get a copy? He said, "The church announced it, and I went on Amazon and bought it."

Then I heard of another lady in our church that bought the book to give to her friend, who is not a mom. "But," she said, "The book isn't just for moms. It will encourage anyone."

Now *I'm* encouraged.

Something else encouraging, I have battled the most intolerable aching legs. I'm not sure of the cause, but I struggled with it all last week, and then today, it lifted. A lack of food or water could be the reason. Or perhaps the way I hold Eden on my legs is cutting off circulation. But today was a great day in terms of health. I'm thanking God for the relief. Also, the ringing in my ears is more tolerable than it has been in three years, and I can only attribute it to answered prayer.

Thank you, Lord, for good days as they sure are fleeting. Teach us ways to redeem the time for Your glory. Passing out tracts wherever I go is a favorite way of mine. Plus limiting time on social media and TV (which I don't watch typically). May God show us even more ways.

"Those who have insight will shine brightly like the brightness of the expanse of heaven, and those who lead the many to righteousness, like the stars forever and ever."

Daniel 12:3

"But now having been freed from sin and enslaved to God, you derive your benefit, resulting in sanctification, and the outcome, eternal life."

Romans 6:22

*S*eptember 17, 2019

Eden prayed for Mickey Mouse to watch our film, UnpopularTheMovie.com. She handed a card to him at Disneyland with the link to the website. We forgot to give one to Goofy, and Minnie Mouse didn't get one either as she was too busy to get a picture with us and had to go dance in the streets. Eden prayed Mickey would share it with the others, and they would become Christians. She already knew that they were people wearing costumes, and I realize that sounds like spoiling the fun, but if we tell her the truth now, there will not be heartbreak later. She will know the truth early, and it will set her free.

Isn't it wonderful how, when we walk in the light, we don't have to cover-up darkness? And when we walk in truth, we don't have to cover our tracks in a web of lies. Being faithful and true to the One whose name is Faithful and True is no small thing.

"But now having been freed from sin and enslaved to God, you derive your benefit, resulting in sanctification, and the outcome, eternal life."

Romans 6:22

"But be kind to each other, tenderhearted, forgiving one another just as God also forgave you in Christ."

—Ephesians 4:32

September 21, 2019

How quickly I can be moved. I endeavored for today to be a day focused on "giving thanks with a grateful heart," and promptly hit some roadblocks. One had to do with real estate, which was resolved within an hour. Eden became irritable during that time, but we soon moved on with joy as if nothing happened. I read stories to her, and we laughed. Sadly, our good time did not last. Eden protested to a few things that I told her she couldn't do. I felt my no's to her were said very nicely, but it seemed she was resolved to protest.

My mom was here during all of this, so after I gently instructed Eden, I let them play together while I cleaned the house and tried to clean up my heart. I talk to the Lord about her outbursts which help lift the burden. After an hour of cleaning, I noticed she didn't have one issue with my mom. So, I racked my brain as I wiped the countertops thinking, "Was I wrong in my approach or tone?" I was at a loss, and the nicer Eden was to my mom, the more I felt like Martha in Luke 10 except I was saying, "Lord, don't you care that Eden wasn't nice to me? Tell her to come be nice to me."

Remember Martha grew upset as her sister Mary sat and listened to Jesus while she cleaned in the kitchen. Jesus and Mary may even have been laughing at things. The more they talked and the louder they got, the louder Martha's anger became.

What amazes me is that the God-man Jesus Christ was in Martha's home, yet Martha wasn't at His feet too! She must have not really known who He was. But the text seems to indicate she did know, and she just didn't have time for Him or was too upset over being left to do things on her own that she wouldn't humble herself. How we do the same thing. We make time for other things, but not Him. The person that should have been fuming was the Lord, not Martha; He had the right to be upset at her for putting something like dirt and dishes before Him.

As I was getting upset over the fact that I seem always to take the brunt of Eden's sinful attitude, it helped to see the Lord's compassionate response to Martha. He genuinely seemed to correct her in love. The One who was due full respect and honor from Martha humbled himself and went to her to gently instruct her.

It's my goal to deal immediately with issues that arise so that peace will be maintained. But there are times that I still hang on to unforgiveness or allow bitterness to grow. As if to say, "I do more for you than anyone, how dare you treat me this way." Jesus could have said those same words to Martha, but didn't. I decided before bed to have a more serious talk with Eden about her attitude. I asked her if what she did tonight with her protesting was a sin. She said, "Yes."

I said, "You did that a lot. Which means you have a lot of sin. What are you going to do about it?"

She said, "Welp....trust Jesus."

Her response was so sweet I almost cried. But her sin can be equally as terrible. Since the level of her protests has increased, I decided that the level/intensity of my gospel presentation should too. I'm not sure how much she will remember, but I asked her, "Do you trust Jesus? Have you done it yet?" To which she says, "no." At one point, I told her that young people and young children die too, and her eyes got huge. And said that she is not too young to get saved. That salvation is not just for older people, but for children also. The last thing I want to do is overwhelm her or take away from her childhood fun. However, I know that she gets tons and tons of play/fun time (she has two rooms in our home one for play and one for more play/school time), so perhaps the Lord was leading in this more urgent approach.

After our talk, she got up from my lap and said, "I've been tending to a plant in the backyard, and it grew a flower for you." She pretended to pick it and present it to me. I waited till she closed her eyes to let the tears fall.

Through all of this, God also dealt with me and my attitude. Anger may help to accomplish a lot of cleaning, but it won't achieve the righteousness of God (Ephesians 4:22-24). In other words, when I am angry or have bitterness stirring, I can begin cleaning the house like crazy. (I'm sure Martha's anger turned her into a lean, mean cleaning machine.) But it falls short of the holiness of God, which is true cleanliness.

"But be kind to each other, tenderhearted, forgiving one another just as God also forgave you in Christ."

⇒Ephesians 4:32

⤚ FEET ⤙

*S*eptember 23, 2019

I think I'm beginning to see an answer to my prayers for Eden to be more kind and affectionate. For example, I recently was downcast, and Eden started to lift my spirits by praising my work, saying, "Mama, thank you for vacuuming," and "I love you." And then saying, "Can you cuddle me? I want milk forever." And I wish I could give her milk forever. All nursing moms probably understand that.

I'm also beginning to wonder if Eden is more of an introvert. She tends to clam up in crowds and say, "Mama, I'm shy." Whereas when she is with those she is comfortable with, she talks up a storm.

She also seems to prefer to be at home. We will be out, and in the middle of our time, she will say, "Can we just go home?" I don't mind one bit if she is a homebody, and the thought of Eden ever moving out is incomprehensible. So, I'll cast that care on the Lord (1 Peter 5:7).

Tonight Eden and I painted my mom's nails. I brought over an outfit for her to wear to church too. She said that no one has ever done that for her before. The thought of that can make me cry. We had much fun, and Eden was so serious about the painting that it was too much for my eyes to bear, and my mom was adorable receiving it. She has been to a salon once in her life, and that's it.

I've been to the nail salon many times, but it's still a rare treat. Like today, we went, and Eden picked out polish for me, which matched her bright pink dress. The lady who did  my feet was so sweet and seemed to take her time even though I got the cheapest pedicure available. Jesus knew what he was talking about when he said if the feet are clean, then the whole body feels clean (John 13:10). I'm sure that is why all these nail salons never go out of business. There were a lot of feet to clean in the Lord's time, and there still are. I decided to pick out a pink dress for Eden to wear to church to match my toes. She laughed at that. I think I'll teach her tomorrow that the feet that God thinks are beautiful are not necessarily the ones that are clean and painted and pretty, but rather he thinks beautiful feet are those that bring the good news of the Gospel to people (Romans 10:15).

Whatever the condition of your feet, perhaps this week, beautify them by passing out tracts or talking to someone about the Lord, which reminds me of a little girl about Eden's age that had a horrible fit for her mom and grandma outside the nail salon. The grandma was preaching to the child saying something like, "The Lord is not pleased with that. Jesus can help you." I gave them tracts and told them that I would pray for their little girl." I must say that that grandma's feet were beautiful.

"How lovely on the mountains, are the feet of him who brings good news, Who announces peace and brings good news of happiness, who announces salvation, and says to Zion, "Your God reigns!"

Isaiah 52:7

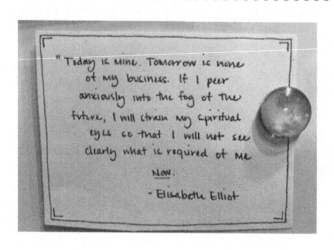

"Today is mine. Tomorrow is none of my business. If I peer anxiously into the fog of the future, I will strain my spiritual eyes so that I will not see clearly what is required of me now.

— Elisabeth Elliot

"Are not two sparrows sold for a cent? And yet not one of them will fall to the ground apart from your Father. "But the very hairs of your head are all numbered. "So do not fear; you are more valuable than many sparrows."

⇁Matthew 10:29-31

*S*eptember 24, 2019

As I was getting ready for church and put on an outfit that I've worn many times. When Eden saw me as she walked around the kitchen corner, she said, "Mama, you look pretty." The two people that compliment me the most are my mom and Eden. Life sure would be dull without them. My mom notices everything new or old or whatever on me. Since I'm her 42-year-old child, she has her eyes set on me more than anyone else. Those of us that are children of God have a Heavenly Father who watches us even closer than my mom watches me. That can be an incredible comfort for the child of God. And not so much of a comfort for a child of darkness that is not living in the light. Today if you are reading this and you are walking in darkness and don't like and are not comforted by the thought of God always watching you then I'd encourage you to cry out to Him today for mercy. Just ask Him to change you. He will not turn you away. You have His Word on it. In John 6:37 Jesus says that "All that the Father gives Me will come to Me, and the one who comes to Me I will certainly not cast out."

"Are not two sparrows sold for a cent? And yet not one of them will fall to the ground apart from your Father. "But the very hairs of your head are all numbered. "So do not fear; you are more valuable than many sparrows."

⇁Matthew 10:29-31

"Let us not lose heart in doing good, for in due time we will reap if we do not grow weary."

Ephesians 6:9

S*eptember 25, 2019*

Emilio sent me a text message that said, "Keep memorizing with Eden." And something of the effect of "Don't give up and don't take it for granted." I was thankful for the encouragement. Although Eden had not indicated that she was tired of all the singing, I had begun to wonder if she was growing weary.

Emilio's text encouraged me to keep going, so I picked up the iPad and recorded a song in my voice singing all of Romans chapter 8. The tune I sang was one that I had created before Eden was born. My plan was a simple one: hit the play button throughout the day and let her listen. After two days of doing this, I quizzed Eden and was quite surprised by what she remembered. I said, "I'm going to sing the verses, and when I stop, you help me fill in the word." So I started, "Therefore, there is now no..." And she said, "condemnation." So, I keep singing, and she kept filling in, word after word. I was amazed at what her two-year-old brain held.

All of this to say, we never know what is in the heart of a person or how weary they may be. A kind word of encouragement can be all that's needed to keep someone pressing on, and into, the things of God. In fact, in Hebrews 3:13 it says, but encourage one another day after day, as long as it is still called "Today," so that none of you will be hardened by the deceitfulness of sin." What a wonderful reminder. We need encouragement day to day. Not month to month or even week to week but day to day. Who will you encourage today? Is there someone in your very own home that could use a word of encouragement? Someone in your immediate family or at church? Let's put Hebrews 3:13 in practice today.

Eden and Mama at Heritage Grace Community Church

"Let us not lose heart in doing good, for in due time we will reap if we do not grow weary."

⇒Ephesians 6:9

❧ DIRECTION ❧

"Though each of the peoples may walk in the name of his god, yet we will walk in the name of the LORD our God forever and ever."

Micah 4:5

S

eptember 26, 2019

I helped a dear family that moved here from Colorado to buy a new home. The deal closed last Thursday, after about five months of working to help the family. Eden came along for everything. Every walkthrough, every inspection, even the closing. On the day of the closing, we gave the family a sign to hang in their new home that said:

As for me and my house, we will serve the Lord. Joshua 24:15

As soon as they read the verse, they said, "This is perfect because we had a sticker that said the same thing on our wall in Colorado." I love how God directs our steps like this. And I was grateful to close my first real estate deal. Now, seemingly, the Lord has brought me another client right away.

A couple found our church after moving here from Arizona, and even though they were locked into a lease their heart was to be in a new home. I enjoy selling new homes the most. I think the Lord might be into new things too. After all, he has made us new creatures in Christ (2 Corinthians 5:17), is preparing to create a new heaven and new earth (Revelation 21:1), and to make all things new. (Revelation 21:5) I pray for God to give this new couple peace of mind in all their house making decisions. I pray for you too, dear reader, that whatever your hands find to do, you will acknowledge God and that He will direct your path (Proverbs 3:4-6). Amen.

"Though each of the peoples may walk in the name of his god, yet we will walk in the name of the LORD our God forever and ever."

═Micah 4:5

"The eyes of all look to You, and You give them their food in season."

≈Psalm 145:15

*S*eptember 27, 2019

Today was a great day. Eden and I stayed home and played and read and chased each other around the house on Eden's little scooters. It was much fun and a good workout to boot. I was blessed with a lot of energy today, which I take advantage of with maximum enjoyment. If you battle fatigue or thyroid problems, you understand what I mean.

We also went over to my mom's house to encourage her because she had a vein procedure done yesterday. We had a delightful time dancing and singing and jumping on her mini-trampoline. We also took some time to all pray together. My prayer request was for continued energy to be able to clean more thoroughly. I felt I hadn't really cleaned my home deeply in weeks. That prayer was answered when we got home. I cleaned Eden's room (with her help) and moved things around and decluttered. It was fun, and Eden appreciated all the free space to run around. I'm beginning to wonder if my energy came from the gluten-free, egg-free, dairy-free chocolate chip cookies I ate at my mom's. Maybe I should make those a part of my daily diet. I gave Eden a little cookie too, and she was full of energy also. While we cleaned, I played the Romans 8 song I talked about earlier, and Eden sang it in warp light "cookie" speed.

Later that night, rather out of the blue, Eden said of spicy food, "You won't like spicy. It's sort of like a serpent, but dif-

ferent." I laughed so hard. That may not be the dictionary defi-
nition, but it should be.

*"The eyes of all look to You, and You give them their food in
season."*

—Psalm 145:15

❧ COMPLETION ❧

"Therefore if you have been raised up with Christ, keep seeking the things above, where Christ is, seated at the right hand of God."

Colossians 3:1

*S*eptember 28, 2019

Eden was so sweet again today. I took her to my mom's house, where she had fun jumping on the mini-trampoline. Jumping on the trampoline is something she has done since she could walk (literally). I feel as if I have watched her grow on there. While I was delighting in watching her, I had such a picture in my mind of how the Lord must delight in watching us grow after our new birth. God gives us our second birth and delights in us as He begins a good work that He will bring to completion (Philippians 1:6), which is something we earnestly hope and pray He will do in all of our children as well. Likely we will not see that work completed in them because the Lord will take us home first, but what a relief to know we don't have to start or finish anything. We just sit back and delight in God delighting in His work.

Delighting is something I need to work on in general. Because I write so often, I've noticed a pattern about myself. Every month, during "that time" of the month, great waves of sadness hit me because of Eden's growth.

But this month, I noticed a difference. The sadness wave was significantly less, and I believe it was due to a good distraction of helping a client finalize and close on a home. I just didn't have free space in my mind to "go there" and cry endlessly. I know it seems crazy to think that a mom of a two-year-old could have free time to do anything, but if you know me, I'll make a way to cry somehow. And I'm proof that idleness can breed sad thoughts and regrets. That's why the Proverbs 31 woman "looks well to the ways of her household and does not eat the bread of idleness." One commentary says of this verse,

"As Almighty God, from His lofty watch-tower in heaven, observes all the minutest details of the manifold work that is going on in the busy hive of earth, so does she from her exalted position in which He has placed her, as mistress of the family, and as responsible to Him, observe 'the ways of her household.'"

And after reading that lofty quote my prayer is "God help me!" Can I get an amen?

"Therefore if you have been raised up with Christ, keep seeking the things above, where Christ is, seated at the right hand of God."

—Colossians 3:1

✑ JOYFUL ✑

"Shout joyfully to the LORD, all the earth; Break forth and sing for joy and sing praises."

═Psalm 98:4

*S*eptember 29, 2019

Eden said, "I want to play Mary Had A Little Lamb." She meant on the piano. When I first started teaching her how to play the song, I didn't think she was interested, but she proved me wrong by playing a good portion of the song.

While we were in the piano room, I got my guitar out and began playing different songs like Matt Redman's "Bless The Lord Oh My Soul" and others such as "Go Tell It On The Mountain." We made a joyful noise together as loud as ever. It was a sweet moment. Eden began swaying back and forth while holding Minnie Mouse and sang seemingly from the heart. She also has seemingly been praying more from the heart. Just today, she prayed for the two boys down the street that they "would come to know" the Lord. Amen to that, and Eden too.

A thought after Emilio's sermon today:

Two items were on the veil that was torn when Jesus died: stars and cherubim.

And as you know, everything in the Bible has significance.

The stars represented Jesus as High Priest passing through the heavens, and the cherubim elude back to the Garden of Eden where two cherubim were stationed outside with flaming fire, guarding against anyone entering Eden and eating of the tree of life. When Jesus died on the cross and passed through the heavens, he also passed through the fire of the cherubim, extinguishing God's wrath so to speak.

Think of it like this; Jesus was the ultimate fireman. He was able to extinguish God's wrath for us so that we will be able to eat of the tree of life. Now every time I read about the veil it will be with new eyes. And I don't think I'll ever think of the two angels again the same with the burning fire guarding the way to the garden. What a great High Priest we have in Christ (Heb 6:20, Heb 7:26).

And tonight would be a great night to light a fire in the fireplace and be reminded of these truths if only we didn't live in Texas where it's 96 degrees today.

"Shout joyfully to the LORD, all the earth; Break forth and sing for joy and sing praises."

Psalm 98:4

"My help comes from the LORD, the Maker of heaven and earth."

Psalm 121:2

S

eptember 30, 2019

Emilio was so tired from waking up early and having a full day at church yesterday that he went to bed way before Eden and I. As I went to put Eden down for the night I had all but forgotten about him, but she had not and said, "Goodnight, Papa." And then added, "I wonder if he can hear me?" I said, "Well, God can." And she said, "Goodnight, God." It was so dear.

You have probably heard of the children's book, *Goodnight Moon*. Eden has a copy of it and I owned a copy when I was teaching children back twenty years ago. I thought often of how I wished it had been titled Goodnight God. I would love to do a children's book with a similar feel to that book, but with so much more purpose and meaning. I don't want to teach Eden to talk to the moon. Instead, I want to teach her to speak to the Maker of the moon. That would be a good title too: Goodnight Moon-Maker.

Before bed Eden was pretending to be on the phone and said, "Hmmm...I think my phone is malfunctioning." I cracked up. I have never taught her to say that, but she picks up on everything I do, good and bad.

For example, she has started this funny sniffle thing, and I thought she might be getting a cold. I realized that wasn't the case after it dawned on me that I sniffle a lot. It's just a weird habit that I've since been trying to break, which has been hard. I need the Lord's help not to sniffle. If you ever see me do it please tell me to stop. I should tell Eden to imitate me as I imitate Christ (1 Corinthians 11:1), and I'm confident He didn't have a sniffling problem.

On a different note, I wonder if being a realtor has helped me to be a better mom. It sounds strange, but realty has brought much joy to our family this past month and has been a bit of an adventure to see who and when God will bring the next person to help. I've learned for now by God's grace I can do what the job entails and pour into Eden at the same time. I bring her along for everything, and she does pretty well. Maybe that has to do with the gifts she gets from the homebuilders and lenders along the way. Either way, it's been a wonderful journey so far.

"My help comes from the LORD, the Maker of heaven and earth."

—Psalm 121:2

"As for God, His way is perfect; The word of the LORD is proven; He is a shield to all who trust in Him."

⚘Psalm 18:30

O
ctober 1, 2019

Tonight, after reading *Don't You Feel Well, Sam?* Eden started laughing hysterically. The book is about a little bear that is very sick. At the end of the story, he and his mama sit on the stairs and wait for snow. I told Eden that we should pray for snow this year and that Meesie (my mom) has been telling the Lord for the past two years, "Please do not let it snow." Eden cracked up at the thought that my mom would instruct God in such a way. But interestingly enough, it has not snowed for the past two years.

I, however, am praying that this year it will snow so that Eden and I can make a snowman. It will be fun to see whose prayer gets answered. And I will be very upset if it's not mine. Ha!

Psalm 147:16-18

He gives snow like wool;

He scatters the frost like ashes.

He casts forth His ice as fragments;

Who can stand before His cold?

He sends forth His word and melts them;

He causes His wind to blow and the waters to flow.

Psalm 148:7-8 NASB

Praise the Lord from the earth,
Sea monsters and all deeps;
Fire and hail, snow and clouds;
Stormy wind, fulfilling His word

Proverbs 25:13

Like the cold of snow in the time of harvest
Is a faithful messenger to those who send him,
For he refreshes the soul of his masters.

Proverbs 31:21

She is not afraid of the snow for her household,
For all her household are clothed with scarlet.

Isaiah 1:18

"Come now, and let us reason together,"
Says the Lord,
"Though your sins are as scarlet,
They will be as white as snow;
Though they are red like crimson,
They will be like wool.

"As for God, His way is perfect; The word of the LORD is
proven; He is a shield to all who trust in Him."

⟊Psalm 18:30

∽ PREDESTINED ∽

"He predestined us to adoption as sons through Jesus Christ to Himself, according to the kind intention of His will, to the praise of the glory of His grace, which He freely bestowed on us in the Beloved."

⇒Ephesians 1:5-6

*O*ctober 2, 2019

One of our church members, Krystell, posted these very touching words on my Facebook page.

At 16 years old, I met a married couple in my former place of work. They both would become regulars, and each opportunity they had, they would preach the gospel to me. Something that at that time I rejected due to the church hurt I was experiencing (I didn't know then that's what it was) and the unbelief in my hardened heart. They took every opportunity they had to share the gospel with me. I liked them, but I didn't like the fact that they would tell me the same thing over and over again. A few times, I would hide in the back when I saw them come in. Lol. I know...I was terrible. I quit that job at 20 years old. At 23 years of age, my now-husband, who was my boyfriend at the time, took me to his church to visit. Our entire relationship was long distance, I lived in San Antonio, and he was here in Fort Worth. When I walked into his church, the first person I saw in the nursery was Trisha Ramos, the wife of the couple that would preach to me at work. I jumped up and ran to hug her. That same day, I heard her husband (Emilio) preach. I was surprised, but not.

After all, they did share the gospel non-stop with me.

At 28 years of age, I am married to Sebastian (Pastor Emilio married us). Today we are members of his church, and we have a beautiful and beloved daughter who Trisha is holding in this photograph.

I am beyond thankful to the Lord. He surrounded me with people who love Him to reach me. I can't express my gratitude for my dear friend and sister in Christ, Trisha, and her husband. If at 16 years old, someone had told my old "atheist" self that this would be my life today, and I would be posting this post, I would have laughed in their face. I'm humbled because I don't deserve any of it. But God is so merciful to take away what we deserve and give us what we don't, salvation. (Ephesians 1:5)

"He predestined us to adoption as sons through Jesus Christ to Himself, according to the kind intention of His will, to the praise of the glory of His grace, which He freely bestowed on us in the Beloved."

Ephesians 1:5-6

⤙ SOFT ⤚

O
ctober 3, 2019

We are memorizing Proverbs 15:1, *"A soft answer turns away wrath."* I use it in a disarming way with Eden when she is about to get upset over not getting her way. I quote the verse and say, "If you say, "No!" In a mean way to mama, then you will bring the wrath of the pow pow (rod) to yourself. But if you have a sweet answer and say, "No, mama." Or "No, thank you, Mama," then your soft answer will turn away the wrath of the pow pow." Incorporating the verse in this new way has helped Eden to stop and say sorry quickly and change her tone.

Never have I thought of that verse in that light before. Typically the meaning is regarding an argument, and that kind words diffuse anger in others. So the next time tempers rise, remember Proverbs 15:1 and apply it with confidence.

∾ PROVISION ∾

"Out of the mouth of babes and nursing infants, You have ordained strength..."

≡Psalms 8:2

*O*ctober 4, 2019

I read this lovely testimony from Lina, a missionary friend, tonight before bed. It's special when things like this happen. God is near to His children.

"TESTIMONY OF THE LORDS GOODNESS: I was going through my recipe books today to meal plan for Josef's lunch for the next few days, and I came across a recipe that I wanted to make him. I didn't get to go grocery shopping tonight for basil (which I needed) because Josef got home later than usual. So I scratched that off my menu and all day and part of the night passed, and I couldn't think of what to replace this entree with. Josef had no idea I was in need of basil, and neither was anyone except the Lord and I! Anyways, just now Josef told me, "Hey, there's a basil plant in the car, can you go get it?" What! Turns out, he got it today at his seminary's food pantry! In the year of being here, I've never seen any herbs there, but today the Lord had a special gift for us! This month marks 12 years that I waved to my loved one's goodbye with tears running down my face, crying for hours in the car, not knowing if I would ever see them again. We were on a mission to preach Christ and Him crucified to a nation that was not our own. We didn't know the future, not knowing where we would live or how we would eat and make ends meet. But we knew one thing that we serve a faithful God! We knew that if He called us to ministry, then He would provide! Twelve years later He's still providing in the most miraculous ways!"

Amen to that.

Then today, Eden said the sweetest thing. There were big ants in her bedroom, and she said, "I hope they find their mama."

"Out of the mouth of babes and nursing infants, You have ordained strength..."

Psalms 8:2

"I have hidden Your word in my heart that I may not sin against You."

≈Psalm 119:11

October 5, 2019

This week has been fun. Eden and I have been memorizing verses that correspond with the ABC's. For example:

A soft answer turns away wrath. Proverbs 15:1

Blessed are the peacemakers, for they shall be called sons of God. Matthew 5:9

Children, obey your parents in all things, for this is well-pleasing to the Lord. Colossians 3:20

Do all things without complaining and disputing. Philippians 2:14

Even a child is known by his deeds. Proverbs 20:11

For God so loved the world that he gave his only begotten Son, that whosoever believes in him shall not perish but have everlasting life. John 3:16

I got the idea from a clever book called *My ABC Bible Verses, Hiding God's Word In Little Hearts* by Susan Hunt. And because my brain is slow and since through trial and error I've learned memorizing to song is the best and quickest way to get something into your brain and

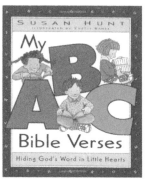

keep it there, I made tunes to most of the verses and recorded them on my phone and I'll play them while we walk along the way or eat food or are in the car or whenever we can. What a fantastic way for both of us to redeem the time while Eden learns the alphabet. You can try it too.

"I have hidden Your word in my heart that I may not sin against You."

—Psalm 119:11

☙ PATIENCE ❧

"Pray in the Spirit at all times, with every kind of prayer and petition. To this end, stay alert with all perseverance in your prayers for all the saints."

⇒Psalm 119:11

*O*ctober 6, 2019

It's a rare treat for Eden to play with my cellphone, and when she does, I make sure it's on Airplane Mode. Today she wanted to use it to "write" while talking into the microphone like she sees me do whenever sending a text. Here is what her entry looked like:

"I would like to say I would like to say that I was going to read ;&&;$&:&:&@@@:@@&:' dkldkdjhxhuhddjjdjkdkjdkddmbdh pew thatbnsbq answer the door when it's called I want it OK child is known by his known by beats, Watch children,, are you obey your parents all things and unload cute,hajjajjjsjbjjnjJZjjjkjiSJa I am Anna mama what's Sabi said the mom Candi are you a mess she said the mama I'm currently by Canyon by Apple I watch me something and I'll see you there he thought of the Philippians 410 to 14 to Fisher of Kim 214 I love afternoon afternoon after that Meesie what's your shake your Waipio it's yours I'll pay you something and you paid is it never said he'll miss you Paris something nowhbeatshdsjjhshhhdhhhsjjhjsjjwjiwksjjßjjsjsjaajSjjAjjabus OK byejjj"

It was so funny to read, as her speech had been as clear as day to me, but my cellphone obviously couldn't understand her. This makes me think of God and how He knows how to make sense of our jumbled hearts and knows how to precisely minister His Word to us. And He is perfectly patient even when our theology might be off. It took me years to get where I am now theologically, and He was gently leading all along the way. Maybe we can learn a lesson or two from Him with our children when they are not where we think they should be in their learning or manners or biblical knowledge. I know I can quickly forget that Eden is only two years and ten months old. It is also a comfort to know that when we don't know what to pray or if we just can't seem to articulate all that is in the deepest parts of our heart we know that God says the "Spirit Himself intercedes for us with groaning too deep for words (Romans 8:26).

Tomorrow I want to slow down a bit and just enjoy the day. I say that because we read a lot of books today, about 12-15. And I had a lady ask me if I was a teacher as I was returning about 20 books at the library. I thought, "Well, no....but, yes, to Eden." I tried to say that in so many words, but it probably sounded crazy, so I just gave her a gospel tract, which I'm sure further confirmed in her mind my craziness.

"Pray in the Spirit at all times, with every kind of prayer and petition. To this end, stay alert with all perseverance in your prayers for all the saints."

—Psalm 119:11

⤛ FREE ⤜

"So Jesus was saying to those Jews who had believed Him, "If you continue in My word, then you are truly disciples of Mine; and you will know the truth, and the truth will make you free."

≡John 8:32

*O*ctober 7, 2019

Eden almost always wants to stay in her room for as long as humanly possible. So, I'll say something like, "Just a few more minutes, and we will get ready for bed." And she will say, "May we please stay longer?" But tonight was a bit different. I looked at all the library books on the floor and said, "You know what Eden, we have spent a lot of time in other books today, and I want us to spend time in the book that is good for our souls. These books are fun and all, but we need to read the bible to get our souls right and adjusted and fed. Remember that the bible is food for the soul." I was a bit surprised when she said, "Let's go." I might try saying that to her more often. After all, it's the truth, and the truth will set us free (John 8:32).

"So Jesus was saying to those Jews who had believed Him, "If you continue in My word, then you are truly disciples of Mine; and you will know the truth, and the truth will make you free."

≡John 8:32

❧ LEAD ❧

"The LORD knows the way of the righteous, but the way of the wicked will perish."

Psalm 1:6

O*ctober 8, 2019*

Shoes have been a real issue today. Eden pushes back and grumbles when I suggest she wear certain shoes. So today, when we were reading a book about a dog called "Tiny," I pointed out a picture of a group of dogs on leashes and how all the dogs were ahead of the people and walking them, but it should be the other way around. The people should be walking the dogs not the dogs walking the people. She paid very close attention as she used her tiny finger to point things out in the book. I then said, "It's like us, should you be leading me?" She shook her head and laughed as if to say "no." So today, when she wanted to lead me and tell me what she was going to do and which shoes she was going to wear, I reminded her what happened the last time she did things her way. She fell off her scooter and cut her foot because she had flip flops on and not the shoes I had suggested. Then I said, "Are you leading Mama?" She smiled and said, "No." and kept her shoes on for our whole walk.

I've also been telling her to take note just how easy it is to grumble and complain. The words just roll off the tongue, and that I need to be on guard as well. I told her if she hears me grumbling and complaining to encourage me with the verse from Philippians 2:14, "Do all things without grumbling or disputing." I explained that I grumble less than she does because I have a new heart, and the Holy Spirit helps me. Today in her prayers she said, "please change my heart, God." Amen.

"The LORD knows the way of the righteous, but the way of the wicked will perish."

⸗Psalm 1:6

✢ TENDERHEARTED ✢

"Bearing with one another, and forgiving each other, whoever has a complaint against anyone; just as the Lord forgave you, so also should you."

—Colossians 3:13

O
ctober 9, 2019

Tonight I was reflecting on forgiveness and how, when we sin or error in our parenting, it can be hard to pick up and walk in joy quickly. Our children seem to move on from things much faster. But a wonderful verse that I happened upon today while reading to Eden out of a book called *Everyone A Child Should Know*. My eyes landed on Psalm 103:4 "But with you there is forgiveness, so that we can, with reverence, serve you." What a verse. There may not be forgiveness found in anyone else, but there is forgiveness found in the Lord so that He may be honored and revered and feared and served.

Amazingly, forgiveness and service go hand in hand. Forgiveness frees our minds and hands to do God's work with joy. The exact opposite is true of unforgiveness, which paralyzes and causes a lack of any good fruit.

Then tonight before bed Eden was instructing her little Minnie Mouse, who was having trouble wanting to keep her shoes on, telling her, "Minnie, I have a verse for you...'Be kind to one another, tenderhearted forgiving one another, as God in Christ forgave you'" (Ephesians 4:32).

I was blessed hearing that verse. I had forgotten I had taught it to her, and I needed it tonight.

That tenderhearted verse is for all moms, though. Our hearts can become hardened quickly by serving endlessly and receiving very little affirmation or thanks.

Lord, we need your help to be kind to the "one anothers" in our own homes. We need Your grace to do so. Your daily grace. We don't want to have hardened hearts. Sin is deceitful, and as Hebrews 3:13 says, we should encourage one another daily, so that the deceitfulness of sin doesn't harden our hearts. Amen.

"Bearing with one another, and forgiving each other, whoever has a complaint against anyone; just as the Lord forgave you, so also should you."

=Colossians 3:13

"God is Light, and in Him there is no darkness at all."

⇒1 John 1:5

*O*ctober 10, 2019

I decided to record a little jingle for the verse, *"Charm is deceptive, and beauty is vain, but a woman who fears the Lord is worthy to be praised"* (Proverbs 31:30). I played it a couple times on my phone, and about 30 minutes later, I heard Eden singing it in the back of the car.

Then I recorded another jingle for Romans 10:15, *"How beautiful are the feet of those who preach good news."* I played it in the background as Eden and I acted out little dramas of what to do when children knock on our door on Halloween. I have been teaching her the difference between Reformation Day, Harvest, and Halloween. She seems to be identifying in the neighborhood the things that are for Harvest versus the things that are for Halloween. In fact, on our walk tonight, we came upon a home that had some rather scary Halloween decorations. Eden took one glance at and said, "I cannot look at it" and turned away. Then she started singing loud, "Rejoice, rejoice, rejoice O daughter of Zion! Look at your King come to you! Righteous and having salvation! Humble and riding on a donkey! Zechariah nine nine!"

It reminded me of the time we foolishly took Eden on the Pirates of Caribbean ride at Disneyland. We covered her eyes and she did too the entire time. The imagery on that ride was all darkness, and when we got out of there, she started singing a Christian song as well. I pray she will come to know the difference between light and dark and want to go to the King of Light.

Speaking of the King of Light, tonight I read Eden *The Lightlings* by the late R.C. Sproul (who actually passed away on Eden's 1 year birthday). The story is about little creatures that have wings that light up and is basically the account of Adam and Eve but written in fiction. While reading it, I was reminded of a purple dress my Aunt Vicki bought Eden for Halloween that has wings that light up. She could wear that dress on Halloween as we desire to bring knowledge of the One who is true light to the trick-or-treaters. Rejoice!

"God is Light, and in Him there is no darkness at all."

1 John 1:5

❧ REASONS ❧

"I love the LORD, because he has heard my voice and my pleas for mercy."

Psalm 116:1

*O*ctober 11, 2019

We had lovely weather today. Sunny and very warm for October. We painted in the backyard and sat in the car in the driveway and pretended to drive places. Eden told me she wanted to stay with me in the car all night. Then I got her situated in her car seat to go to the park when she said, "Mama, I love you."

I asked her, "Why do you love me?"

She said, "Cubz, you are a friend to me."

I said, "Why am I a friend to you?"

She said, "Cubz, you were so sweet to me."

It was a touching moment. I'm sure the Lord loves when we tell Him all the reasons why we love Him. Maybe tonight is a good time to do that afresh.

"*I love the LORD, because he has heard my voice and my pleas for mercy.*"

═Psalm 116:1

⤳ COMFORT ⤳

"For the LORD God is a sun and shield: the LORD will give grace and glory: no good thing will he withhold from them that walk uprightly."

⇒Psalm 84:11

*O*ctober 12, 2019

There is a universal language of motherhood. We have a lot of Hindu families in our neighborhood, and I nearly cried and had to hold back the tears while talking to one as I pushed Eden on the swing yesterday. Her son and Eden were almost the exact age. She looked at me, and in her broken English, said, "She is a gem to you, isn't she?" The lady was so sincere and sweet and kind. I made sure to give her tracts as we left. Eden said she wanted to swing all night. And I wanted her to too, like maybe staying in one spot would make time stand-still. Sometimes I busy myself with other things because see-ing her growth can be tremendously painful to my eyes. But I can never stay away too long. Truth is, I want Eden by my side for everything. I enjoy her company.

She's easy to forgive too. I can forgive her 400 times a day, but it's hard for me to receive the grace of God quickly for myself when I am impatient or overcome with grief which can overtake me in seconds. Like today, I had grief. Not over Eden's sins but over how much she seems to have changed. I think she may have picked up on my sadness when she got upset over something small (but big to her). So when Emilio got home, I decided to go on a walk to cry and pray.

I called my mom as I was walking and poured out my heart. I told her I was upset at my sadness and upset that I can't stop the clock and upset over my own failures as a mom. She gave me some verses and said I must get my joy from the Lord. Which I knew, but needed to be reminded of. I also had a deep sadness thinking Eden could be my only child. Emilio thinks raising one child is difficult enough and is content with just Eden. Pray for him, I have a short window of time left. Or maybe pray for me, that I should be content.

After 35 minutes of talking and my mom praying, I was headed home feeling slight relief. I didn't want to go into the house with a sad face, though, but with joy. Then Emilio texted me, saying Eden was crying for me.

What a mess we all are. Ha.

Maybe pray for all of us, that we will all be content.

"For the LORD God is a sun and shield: the LORD will give grace and glory: no good thing will he withhold from them that walk uprightly."

—Psalm 84:11

"For God so loved the world that He gave His one and only Son, that everyone who believes in Him shall not perish but have eternal life."

⇌John 3:16

O
ctober 13, 2019

Tips for overcoming self-pity:

- Take a walk outside to pray (1 Thessalonians 5:17)
- Call your mom or a Christian friend and ask them to pray for you (James 5:16)
- Text, write, or call someone else and pray for them (Hebrews 3:13)
- Go to the store closest to you and pass out gospel tracts (Daniel 12:3)
- Listen to a sermon or message (Colossians 3:1)
- Put on worship till the darkness lifts (Ephesians 5:19)
- Write a list of as many things as you can think of to be thankful for, (Psalm 103:2)

Here's my simple list from today of things I am thankful for:

- The Bible
- My mom and Eden and a husband who has not left me (ha)
- A solid church where I can find encouragement
- That I had food today
- Cooler weather and for a lovely walk with Eden
- That there is forgiveness with the Lord, that He might be feared (Proverbs 9:10)

You get the idea.

A friend mentioned to me tonight how glad she is that she only has one child as it allows her to savor time with just the two of them. She went on to say that her friend, with many children, recently told her that she wished that she had only one child (not that she doesn't love them all). Still, she desired to spend quality time with one, but can't because she has many. Then my friend reminded me that Sarah only had Isaac.

Two hours later, I was still thinking about her message and how Jesus was the only Son of the Father. He was an only child if you will, who the Father shares with us (sinners). It's a radical, earth-shattering truth. "For unto us a child is born, unto us a Son is given" (Isaiah 9:6).

God knows what it's like to have a Son close to Him. In fact, the Father and the Son were/are so close that Jesus said, "If you've seen me, you've seen my Father."

I'm sure as a mom, you love when your child mimics you and follows in your righteous footsteps. What an honor to the Father that Christ did that to the utmost. He never disrespected the Father. Unlike us, Christ obeyed the Father in everything, not to mention how they are in total harmony and union. It breaks my heart when I feel out of union with Eden. Can you imagine the searing pain when the Father turned His face away at the scene of the cross? "As wounds which marred the Chosen One brought many sons to glory" are lyrics taken from the song, *In Christ Alone*. Eden is very sensitive to my moods and nature, and if she ever senses me turn my face away from her, she is in anguish. I try with the help of God to be cheerful and consistent but sometimes fail. God never fails, though.

"For God so loved the world that He gave His one and only Son, that everyone who believes in Him shall not perish but have eternal life."

≈John 3:16

⤚ PLENTY ⤙

"The Lord is my Shepherd, I shall not want."

⤙Psalm 23:1

October 17, 2019

Eden said, "Mama, what church do you go to?" We have a game of pretending we to go to different churches.

Then she said, "I go to Disneyland church."

I bet that is fun!

She has also started to pray for our neighbors that have put up evil-looking Halloween decorations in their yard. She prays that they will "tear them down and throw it away and come to the Lord." Amen. I love hearing her prayers. I can't bring myself to correct her on a few words she mispronounces though. In Eden's world, the word almost is pronounced "alsme"; library is "libraria"; and Sprouts is "souts". I pray I'm not let down the day she says those words correctly.

Speaking of let down, do you get let down when your favorite place to eat is out of a particular item or no longer carries your favorite dessert? I know I do. In heaven, this will never happen. Imagine being at the banqueting table at the Marriage Supper of the Lamb, and the Lord tells you He is out of something. That would be ridiculous. He never runs out of anything. So, trust Him for the things you need today (Psalm 23).

"The Lord is my Shepherd, I shall not want."

Psalm 23:1

"God created the great sea monsters and every living creature that moves, with which the waters swarmed after their kind, and every winged bird after its kind; and God saw that it was good."

Genesis 1:21

*O*ctober 19, 2019

Before bed tonight, I heard Eden singing a song with the words from Philippians 2:14, "Do all things without complaining and disputing." It finally dawned on me that she was singing a tune that she had "written" herself. I couldn't believe it. So, I had her teach it to me. What a turn of events. I've never had a 2-year-old teacher before.

We also had fun continuing to memorize Genesis 1, specifically the creation of day five. We hope to have all of Genesis chapter 1 memorized by the end of the year. It will take some work, but it's good for my soul and hers as well. Eden really seems to like the new tune I made up for day five and the part where God created the "great sea monsters," which is a tremendous help in her learning. Not to mention in keeping her from complaining and disputing.

"God created the great sea monsters and every living creature that moves, with which the waters swarmed after their kind, and every winged bird after its kind; and God saw that it was good."

Genesis 1:21

⤞ REPETITION ⤝

"These words, which I am commanding you today, shall be on your heart. You shall teach them diligently to your sons and shall talk of them when you sit in your house and when you walk by the way and when you lie down and when you rise up."

═Deuteronomy 6:6

*O*ctober 20, 2019

Before bed, Eden had her pink sparkle stroller and was loading it up with all her valuables. She also had on her pink backpack. It was all too cute for my eyes.

She began digging through things and said, mostly to herself, "I'm looking for my phone." Then she added, "It says, 'Blessed are the peacemakers for they shall be called sons of God.'" And then she looked at me square in the eyes and said, "Matthew 5:9." I nearly fell off my seat. I had forgotten that we had memorized that verse. I had even forgotten the tune we used, but somehow in the back of her mind, she dug deep and pulled out the file. What a blessed way to end the day.

"These words, which I am commanding you today, shall be on your heart. You shall teach them diligently to your sons and shall talk of them when you sit in your house and when you walk by the way and when you lie down and when you rise up."

═Deuteronomy 6:6

"The people walking in darkness have seen a great light; on those living in the land of the shadow of death, a light has dawned."

⟨Isaiah 9:2

October 21, 2019

There is a good chance that I'm cutting off the circulation in my legs when I hold Eden during her naptime and at night. And it's causing my legs to have a restless leg syndrome feel. I'm not certain, though, so I dug out my old Boppy pillow and decided to have Eden lay on it instead. She said, "No, Mama, don't use that...I like to feel your tummy." That really touched my heart, so I didn't use the Boppy. My legs may disagree with that decision.

Eden didn't object to putting star stickers on my nails (and hers), though. I'm glad Eden chose the stars as they remind me of the verse in Daniel 12:3 that says, "Those who turn many to righteousness will shine like the stars forever and ever."

As I think about it, our hands were made for much more than star stickers. For example, they can be used to help turn many to righteousness, simply by passing out gospel tracts. Thank God for giving us such a cheap and fun way to redeem the time. If you are reading this and have never passed out a Gospel tract, go to livingwaters.com and buy a pack of 100 for $5. And when they arrive you will be glad they did and so will your neighbor who may be in living in darkness.

"*The people walking in darkness have seen a great light; on those living in the land of the shadow of death, a light has dawned.*"

≡Isaiah 9:2

❧ UNITY ❧

October 22, 2019

I was feeling a bit down today and texted my mom for prayer. No one in my house would have known how I was feeling, and nothing happened per se. It was just the fact that Eden woke up seemingly having another growth spurt and newfound reason and understanding, all of which are good. Still, I ached today with a sense of loss.

I also ached after thinking of my mom's losses. All the things I put her through without even knowing it. I always wondered why she always seemed so broken and sad when I left to go here or there. I'm sure it was because she wanted to go here and there with me. Growing up, she was very committed to me and attended every one of my high school events. Not only that, but she gave me money (that she didn't have) so that I could buy a yearbook every year and not feel left out. She also washed my clothes to such perfection that people would ask me how I got my clothes so white. Our home was just as immaculate.

I never understood why my mom would cry when I would tell her that I wanted to be a truck driver and that she and I would drive the truck, and we would have a lot of animals and I'd never marry. I still remember her tear-filled eyes looking at me while hearing of my plans. However, God had other plans, and she has Eden now as a gift from God.

I'm thankful that God's plans are infinitely better than our own. It's something that I need to remind myself of daily. It also helped when today, Eden told me, "I don't want ever to leave you." It was most special to hear her say that because she had no idea how I had been feeling. I pray God plans for her always to remain close to us, but His will be done.

Later in the day, I had Emilio run an errand to pick up band-aids. He came home with two boxes of the wrong kind. A few days later, he went back for another box and came home again with the wrong type. He said there were so many band-aids to choose from that he didn't know what to pick. As I'm writing this, I almost laughed out loud and woke Eden up. The thought of him having such trouble just cracks me up. He said the outside of the box shows what he wants, but the inside is totally different. The same can be true of finding a good church. Some churches say the right thing and package their websites and doctrinal statements to read biblically, but then you find out the truth when you go inside. I hope God will desire for Eden to attend the same church as Emilio and me. I would love for her and her husband to one day be where we are, under solid, biblical worship and preaching.

Being in a solid church is God's design to strengthen our souls week after week. Just this Sunday, I told Eden that it is important that we listen in church and not be a distraction because people come to church hungry.

I said, "They are not coming hungry for donuts, but they are coming hungry for the Bible to feed their souls."

There is a young woman in our church that is a testimony to the importance of church attendance. She is battling cancer and attends service wearing a mask because her immune system is so weak. She said that her doctor doesn't really want her to go, but she said it has been the best thing for both her health and her soul. That was deeply encouraging to hear. She said after being in the hospital for so long that coming back to church and just one week of fellowship and hearing the word had greatly lifted her spirit. Amen to that.

One last thing…

Today on a walk in the park, we saw a large stone that had Matthew 5:9 written on it, the same verse Eden quoted the other night while playing with her pink sparkle stroller. Help us, Lord, to be faithful peacemakers in our own homes, as well as our children. Like Matthew Henry says of peacemakers: *"They keep the peace that it be not broken, and recover it when it is broken."*

"Behold, how good and how pleasant it is For brothers to dwell together in unity!"

— Psalm 133:1

⤚◈ COVENANT ◈⤙

*O*ctober 23, 2019

I was talking to Eden tonight about John the Baptist baptizing Jesus, and I asked her if Jesus had any sin to be washed away? She said no. So I asked, "Why is he getting baptized then?"

She said, "Please tell me mama, *please* tell me."

I said, "Jesus having no sin to be washed away is another proof that baptism does not wash away sins. Jesus was not going into the water to get his sins washed away, but to fulfill righteousness and obey God and to show the pattern of what His believers will do. His believers will follow this pattern of baptism; to go into the water and show the outward sign of an inward change."

Tonight while in Eden's room, I asked her if she knew what the word "covenant" meant. She didn't, and I've never taught her, so I grabbed two of her stuffed toys and had one pretend to say, "I will never leave you." And the other said, "Me neither." And told her, "A covenant is when two people come to an agreement."

I explained that God made a covenant with Noah and the animals, and He gave the rainbow as a sign that He will never flood the earth again.

Then I had one of the animals pretend to leave and break the covenant, and the other was heartbroken. I told her that

God is not like that. He keeps His promises (unlike man). He is altogether lovely and different.

Perhaps some of you have experienced a broken covenant; through a divorce or some sort of business deal gone bad or a family member no longer talking with you because of your union with Christ. We all have our heartbreaking situations, but when we fix our eyes on things above, as we are exhorted to do in Colossians 3, our perspective changes as we gaze and meditate on the covenant keeper (God). How wonderful it is that He is not like us. That He doesn't change (Malachi 3:6). And He will keep His Word and His name is Faithful and True (Lamentations 3:23-26). What a relief and refuge. Do you feel weak today? Take heart! God is our refuge and strength, a very present help in trouble" (Psalm 46:1).

"But You remain the same, and Your years will never end."

⟭Psalm 102:27

RAINBOW

"I set My bow in the cloud, and it shall be for a sign of a covenant between Me and the earth."

Genesis 9:13

*O*ctober 25, 2019

Eden asked before bed, "Mama, did God flood the earth?" She was pretending to quiz me the way that I quiz her using a most incredible little book called *My 1st Book of Questions and Answers* by Carine Mackenzie. R.C. Sproul endorsed it along with Sinclair Ferguson. It's a short book of about 114 questions.

Then she asked me, "Did God put an end to the earth?" I didn't understand what she was saying, so I asked her what she meant. And she said, "Did God to stop the rain?" She was asking if God stopped the flood and if he would not do it again. I assured her that he would not flood the earth again and He told us so with the rainbow. The rainbow was His sign to us that he would never flood the earth again and He has kept that promise. Is that wonderful? So when you feel as if you are surrounded by covenant breakers (including yourself) then the next time you see a rainbow be encouraged that there is One who will always keep His promises.

"I set My bow in the cloud, and it shall be for a sign of a covenant between Me and the earth."

Genesis 9:13

NUTRITION

"Whether, then, you eat or drink or whatever you do, do all to the glory of God."

1 Corinthians 10:31

*O*ctober 26, 2019

I had a friend ask about foods I eat at home and at restaurants. She is desiring to make changes to her diet by eliminating gluten and dairy.

This is what I wrote to her. May it be a help to you as well especially if you have an auto immune condition or battle low thyroid or have hasimotos.

Keep in mind, I live in Frisco, TX, so some of the places I mention may only be local to me.

However, if you would like to move to here, which is the happiest place on earth (ha!), please contact me. I'm a realtor and would love to help you navigate in finding a home. You can message me on my Facebook page Facebook.com/fishwithtrish or email me at fishwithtrishdotcom@gmail.com.

Now back to food. When eating out, I go to:

Hat Creek Burger Co. I order fries and burger, no bun, add bacon, mushroom, and avocado.

Chick-fil-A. I order the Kid's Meal with grilled nuggets.

Scotty P's. I order grilled chicken (no bun) add bacon, and sweet potato fries (tell them gluten-free).

Chipotle. I order a bowl with rice, guacamole, lettuce, any meat, and salsa.

Pei Wei. I order gluten-free sweet chicken with rice and vegetables.

Best Thai. I order Pad Thai, no egg, and add mushroom and a number 1 spicy (or no spicy at all). It is sooo good.

Everything I laid out for you here is both gluten-free and dairy-free.

This may not sound healthy, but at home, we eat a smoothie almost every day. I also juice a lot too.

We also eat a lot of steamed carrots, zucchini, squash, asparagus, broccoli, and spinach almost daily.

I recently made a smoothie consisting of:

1 apple

1 orange

Some pineapple chunks

Large handful of spinach

Add crushed ice (just handful)

Add water (half cup or so)

Mix everything in Vitamix or a blender and drink.

For desserts:

Necktar for ice cream, it's the best dairy-free and gluten-free dessert place there is in town. They have delicious smoothies too.

Smoothie King. I order the Vegan Nutty Super Grain, add spinach.

Unrefined Bakery. I order the vegan chocolate cupcake. It is the best in my opinion of anywhere.

May you eat all of this (but not all at one time) to the glory of God.

"Whether, then, you eat or drink or whatever you do, do all to the glory of God."

1 Corinthians 10:31

"Help me, O LORD my God; Save me according to Your loving-kindness."

⟜Psalm 109:26

O
ctober 28, 2019

We went out to run errands today, and Eden was having a hard time. I gave her a quick talk about the Gospel and her need for the Lord. I asked her to pray but did not tell her what to say. She prayed, "Lord, I was having a hard time...please save me." Amen

"Help me, O LORD my God; Save me according to Your loving-kindness."

⟜Psalm 109:26

⊰ CHILDREN ⊱

"And calling to him a child, he put him in the midst of them and said, "Truly, I say to you, unless you turn and become like children, you will never enter the kingdom of heaven. Whoever humbles himself like this child is the greatest in the kingdom of heaven."

≡Matthew 18:2-4

*O*ctober 29, 2019

I love this prayer.

"Lord, I pray dogs will be in heaven and that there will be no band aids and no ouches and no darkness." -Eden

Amen to that.

"And calling to him a child, he put him in the midst of them and said, "Truly, I say to you, unless you turn and become like children, you will never enter the kingdom of heaven. Whoever humbles himself like this child is the greatest in the kingdom of heaven."

≡Matthew 18:2-4

❦ THANKSGIVING ❦

"In everything give thanks; for this is God's will for you in Christ Jesus."

1 Thessalonians 5:19

*O*ctober 30, 2019

Throughout the day, I read to Eden from her Children's Bible. We are almost through our third time reading it. I was talking to her about Jesus not having a place to lay His head (not even a rock). And went on to say there was someone else who didn't have a place to put his head either, but I couldn't remember his name when Eden looked at me square in the eye and said, "Jacob." We had talked about a month ago about Jacob dreaming while he laid his head on a rock. All of this made me thankful for my soft pillow. We sure can become discontent with the home we live in if we look around at others too much. But look to Christ. Our Lord didn't even have a place to lay His head, and he was born in a barn. Tonight may we give thanks for God's provisions. Especially for His mercy and grace. Amen.

"In everything give thanks; for this is God's will for you in Christ Jesus."

1 Thessalonians 5:19

❧ REFORMATION ❧

"And He said to them, "Go into all the world and preach the gospel to all creation."

═Mark 16:15

O

ctober 31, 2019

In our home we celebrate Reformation Day and set up a table and fill it with good candy, lots of Gospel tracts and we turn on every single light. On the garage we put a big sign that says "Happy Reformation Day" and we call our home the "House of Light." It's great. Some kids come back for more. And I love how Jesus said to "Go into the world and preach the gospel to every creature." This is a very easy way to go. All you have to do is "go" out your front door and they will come to you.

"And He said to them, "Go into all the world and preach the gospel to all creation."

═Mark 16:15

"Your Word, O LORD, is eternal it stands firm."

⟜Psalm 119:89

November 1, 2019

In Psalm 119:169, the psalmist is talking to the Lord about something that has become a cry for him, and he takes that cry straight to the One that can help. Then he asks God to give him "understanding according to Your Word." Interestingly, the understanding is not of himself or of man's reason or psychology. Instead, he desires understanding that comes from God's Word.

In verse 170, the psalmist cries out for deliverance, perhaps from His enemies, which is a reason to believe that David wrote this psalm since he was a man of many enemies. Do you feel that you have a lot of enemies? Enemies of your soul perhaps? When enemies arise, bring your cry to God. You have His Word on it that vengeance is His. In fact Romans 12:19 says, "Do not avenge yourselves, beloved, but leave room for God's wrath."

In verse 171, he returns to praise "for You teach me Your statutes."

He goes on to request of God that "His hand will be ready to help" (v.173).

What is so interesting about this stanza in Psalm 119 is that the psalmist goes on to say that he delights in God's law but then says "I have gone astray like a lost sheep" and asks God to "seek" him and calls himself God's servant. So it is funny to me that the servant has gone astray like a lost sheep.

As a mom I am sure many of you reading this can agree that you feel as if there are times that you have gone astray. And what I mean by this is perhaps your affections have gone astray or you are consumed with worry or you are lacking joy because your children are growing and your role is changing. Whatever it may be we need the Lord to seek us. To pull us out of whatever thicket or steep ravine that we find ourselves in. Interestingly enough sheep are easily lost, they cannot help themselves to get up if they are on their back (they need the shepherd to do it), and they are known to be devoured quickly by a wolf if the shepherd is not watching during the nighttime hours (or any hour for that matter).

We need the Lord to get us out of our emotional messes. We don't know how at times. But He does. He knows where we are at and what word will help sustain us. Ask yourself these things the next time you are overtaken or are lost in your emotional tornado:

1. Am I loving the Lord and His Word?

2. Am I reading the Bible to sustain me?

3. Am I doing outreach? Reaching out to others to take focus off myself (yourself) ?

4. Am I being thankful for what I have and don't have (like radical poverty and radical persecution ... for now)?

5. Are you in church faithfully (Psalm 120).? The house of God made the Psalmist glad when they said it's time to go to church. Read Psalm 120:1

In Psalm 119:161 the Psalmist is talking about being persecuted by princes. That sounds like a king to me. It makes sense to me that a King would be persecuted by others in authority. And we know David was a King. Which would be another reason why it seems as if David is the one writing this particular psalm. And even though he's been persecuted by some of the highest ranking people in the land during his time, he says that his heart "stands in awe of God's Word." Other translations have said it this way "Princes persecute me without cause but my heart trembles at your Word." So instead of David trembling at his foes He fears God and His Word far more.

And on top of that in the next verse (Psalm 119:162) he says that he rejoices so much at God's Word as if he found a treasure like gold or money. That's really great rejoicing. Imagine that somebody just gave you a check for $10,000. I bet that would cause you to rejoice. You could freely pay off a few bills and maybe live a little bit more comfortably through the year.

Do we (do I) rejoice at God's Word like we would at a large sum of money? Or are there other things that are causing us to rejoice more?

Then He goes on to say in verse 164 that 7 times a day he praises God because of His Word. Wow. When you feel as if you have nothing to give thanks for, think again. Think of this verse. Think of how often the praise is going up to God. Not over material and temporal things or over people on the earth that die and perish, but instead he rejoices over God's Word! No wonder God called David a man after His own heart.

And then in verse 165 he says the most convicting thing of the whole stanza (in my opinion). He says that those who love God's law have "great peace and nothing causes to stumble." Wow. If we are stumbling it is because we are not loving God's law enough. How convicting is that! I'm convicted just writing about it. That is a major reminder for us to be in God's Word more. And for our children to see it.

When was the last time you were on your knees (that is if they don't hurt you) in prayer to the Lord or on your knees reading the Bible? Lord, help us. We need your grace. More grace upon grace. Bless the readers of this book. And thank you Lord that they have made it to almost the end and have not thrown it out. Amen.

"Your Word, O LORD, is eternal it stands firm."

═Psalm 119:89

❧ PREFERENCE ❧

"Be devoted to one another in brotherly love, give preference to one another in honor…"

Romans 12:10

*N*ovember 2, 2019

Today was a busy day.

1. We started reading Eden's Children's Bible for the fourth time and ended up reading 116 pages (don't worry…that sounds like a lot but there are not very many words on each page and she wanted me to keep reading, I kept asking "are you sure you want me to read more?").

2. We went to Lowe's to buy Christmas lights to hang on our house. I ended up buying a little red truck with lights, as well. Eden picked it out because it reminded her of a book we read called *You Can Do It Sam*. It's all about a little bear and his mama and their quest to deliver cookies to their neighbors in their little green truck.

3. Then we swung by Smoothie King for smoothies on our way to visit my mom.

4. I was outside for a bit with the Christmas lights we had just purchased, organizing them for the crew that would hang them up. When I came inside, Eden said, "I was missing you."

A little later she said, "I love you, mama, and I love God."

I said, "Why do you love the Lord and me?"

She said, "Well, you bought me things like the deer and the Mrs. Bear truck, and you take care of me. And God won't run out of food."

I had forgotten that I had bought that little white deer for her. She kissed it tonight approximately 10 times, which is more kisses than she's given me in the past three months.

5. Finally, before bed, Eden pretended to start writing a book on the iPad that she titled Water Book. I asked her what it was going to be about, and she said, "Sunshine and I think a tricycle book." Should be a best seller.

"Be devoted to one another in brotherly love, give preference to one another in honor…"

≈Romans 12:10

"Whatever you do, whether you eat or drink do all to the glory of God."

≈1 Corinthians 10:31

November 8, 2019

We found this most adorable little bakery earlier this evening in Frisco that serves Boba tea and has other wonderful treats and if you zoom in on the sign behind us it says "Amazing Grace." Here pictured is my dear mom and Eden and I. Yum Yum Yum.

"Whatever you do, whether you eat or drink do all to the glory of God."

≈1 Corinthians 10:31

⨾ AMAZING ⨾

"God, who has called you into fellowship with His Son Jesus Christ our Lord, is faithful."

⨾1 Corinthians 1:9

*N*ovember 11, 2019

Eden was playing with this pet Veterinarian vehicle and she was holding onto the heart monitor. And as she had it in her hand she said "I'm holding on" then she added "to His promises." And she looked back at me.

Amen.

Me too Eden, me too.

She was quoting a Chris Tomlin song that says, "I know who goes before me, I know who stands behind, the God of angel armies is always on my side. The one who reigns forever He is a friend of mine. The God of angel armies is always by my side."

And then there's a line that says, "I am holding onto God's promises He is faithful."

Deuteronomy 7:9

> *Know therefore that the LORD your God is God, the faithful God who keeps His covenant of loving devotion for a thousand generations of those who love Him and keep His commandments.*

2 Thessalonians 3:3

> *But the Lord is faithful, and He will strengthen you and guard you from the evil one.*

And then she was walking down the hall by my side and said, "I was lost... But now I'm found."

I said, "What does that mean?"

She said, "Welp...amazing grace."

Amazing indeed...Amazing grace indeed!

"God, who has called you into fellowship with His Son Jesus Christ our Lord, is faithful."

1 Corinthians 1:9

———— ◆ ————

VISIT MANY GOOD BOOKS,
BUT LIVE IN THE BIBLE.
—Charles Spurgeon

———— ◆ ————

⊱ FORGIVEN ⊰

"Be excellent at what is good, be innocent of evil."

≈Romans 16:19

*N*ovember 16, 2019

Eden woke up earlier today and said, "Dear Lord we pray for this world... that they will not put any more skeletons up."

And then I walked into the room and she was singing, "Dear Lord we love you, dear Lord we love you...and we want to be forgiven of our sins."

Can I get an AMEN!!!

"Be excellent at what is good, be innocent of evil."

≈Romans 16:19

⤙ KEEPER ⤚

"Don't fret it only causes harm."

Psalm 37:8

*N*ovember 17, 2019

I've been meditating on being a "keeper in the home" as found in Titus 2 and I'll quote it for contexts sake:

> *"The aged women likewise, that they be in behaviour as becometh holiness, not false accusers, not given to much wine, teachers of good things; That they may teach the young women to be sober, to love their husbands, to love their children, To be discreet, chaste, keepers at home, good, obedient to their own husbands, that the word of God be not blasphemed" (Tit. 2: 3-5).*

I landed upon a rather encouraging and convicting quote from a commentary that said in terms of the phrase "keepers at home":

> *"That they be keepers or managers at home; keep a neat, attractive house that will make her husband and children love home. Christian women should be the best of house-keepers and should be models to all who know them" (A Commentary on the New Testament Epistles, Vol. 10, p. 273).*

The word in the Greek (here I go again using Greek, finally my Koine (Biblical) Greek classes paid off) is "oikourgous" it is only used here in this verse and nowhere else in the New Testament. It has the meaning of "keepers at home", "workers at home" and even as far as "stayers at home." This can be freeing. I think I'll stay at home tomorrow. Ha!

"Don't fret it only causes harm."

~Psalm 37:8

"…You anoint my head with oil; my cup overflows."

⇒Psalm 23:5

*N*ovember 22, 2019

This evening I was stacking cups on top of each other to make a tree and putting an apple at the top, Eden reached over and put her hand on my chin and (speaking of cups) she cupped her hand around my chin. I told her she was acting like this little bear Sam that was very tender with his mama and clapped his hands around her chin. It melted me. My cup was running over.

Then tonight before bed Eden had a bubble bath and we were pretending that it was snowing bubbles on the edge of the bathtub and her cup was running over with snow and she was saying that her "sins could be white as snow." I decided to read her verses on that very thing. It's amazing how many verses there are on the topic of snow (here is what I read to her):

Psalm 51:7 *Purify me with hyssop, and I shall be clean; Wash me, and I shall be whiter than snow.*

Psalm 147:16-18 *He gives snow like wool; He scatters the frost like ashes. He casts forth His ice as fragments; Who can stand before His cold? He sends forth His word and melts them; He causes His wind to blow and the waters to flow.*

Psalm 148:7-8 *Praise the Lord from the earth, Sea monsters and all deeps; Fire and hail, snow and clouds; Stormy wind, fulfilling His word*

Proverbs 25:13 *Like the cold of snow in the time of harvest Is a faithful messenger to those who send him, For he refreshes the soul of his masters.*

Proverbs 31:21 *She is not afraid of the snow for her house-hold, For all her household are clothed with scarlet.*

Isaiah 1:18 *"Come now, and let us reason together," Says the Lord, "Though your sins are as scarlet, They will be as white as snow; Though they are red like crimson, They will be like wool.*

Isaiah 55:10-1 *For as the rain and the snow come down from heaven, And do not return there without watering the earth And making it bear and sprout, And furnishing seed to the sower and bread to the eater; So will My word be which goes forth from My mouth; It will not return to Me empty, Without accomplishing what I desire, And without succeeding in the matter for which I sent it.*

Lamentations 4:7 *Her consecrated ones were purer than snow, They were whiter than milk; They were more ruddy in body than corals, Their polishing was like lapis lazuli.*

Daniel 7:9 *"I kept looking Until thrones were set up, And the Ancient of Days took His seat; His vesture was like white snow And the hair of His head like pure wool. His throne was ablaze with flames, Its wheels were a burning fire.*

Revelation 1:14 *NASB His head and His hair were white like white wool, like snow; and His eyes were like a flame of fire.*

Eden pretending to make Mama steaks out of sand.

My mom and Mike do not have a fireplace in their home so I thought I would surprise them by ordering one on Amazon and I had it delivered to my house and then I had Emilio drop it off and put it into their spare office room (Ompiee's —grandpa's room). It was all supposed to be surprise for my mom. And tonight when my mom walked in the door to visit for an hour at our house Eden looked up at her as she jumped up and down and said, "You know what Messie...Papa left and dropped off the fireplace and put it into Ompiee's room." I could not believe it. We all laughed hard.

"...You anoint my head with oil; my cup overflows."
                                                    Psalm 23:5

GRACE

"The Lord bless you and keep you; the Lord make His face shine on you and be gracious to you; the Lord turn His face toward you and give you peace."

Numbers 6:24-26

November 23, 2019

Tonight after I put Eden to bed I had so many thoughts of how I could be a better mom. My mind said, "You are not doing enough. How much scripture did you attempt to meditate and memorize today?" Then came a swarm of thoughts about all the things I've done wrong as a mom. As I sat holding Eden I mourned for time lost, time wasted and time not well spent. Then I realized that the answer to all of these issues is found in one word. Grace.

For some reason, we (or I) tend to think that being a good mom is attainable. But that would be like saying that we can attain to being a good Christian. Biblically speaking, there really is no such thing because only God is good. He is the only good Christian if you would, and the only good parent. Yet, in all His perfection and goodness, His first two children (Adam and Eve) listened to the enemy and, for lack of better words, slapped Him in the face. Ouch. But if you are a mom, you can relate in a sense (a small sense) to what the Lord must have felt. After all, He prepared for Adam and Eve a perfect home. No doubt you poured your heart into preparing your baby's first room, having in your mind's eye a Garden of Eden sort of experience for your child. It was the beginning of being the best parent and having your child in the perfect setting and then all would be well. But then reality hits and the truth of

Jesus' words when He says, "In this world you will have trouble" (John 16:33) proves us wrong.

Maybe you picked up this book because you are a weary mom with a lot of guilt and heartache from the choices you've made as a parent, not to mention the choices your children have made. All of which can be sinful, but here we go back to the word needed for the hour, grace.

When I think of grace I think of letting go, of resting, and of surrendering. With the distribution of God's grace to our hearts, we should, in turn, be filled with unspeakable gratitude. It reminds me of when I dreadfully have to discipline Eden and she grabs my neck and says, "Mama, please, can you give grace to me?" knowing she will not get what she deserves. I then explain to her that when Jesus died on the cross I was given grace I didn't deserve. I deserved to be on the cross, not Him. He never sinned (1 Peter 2:22), but I have too many times to count. Somehow in our parenting, we think we can attain some sort of super status as a parent. We want to be in an extraordinary category, especially in the mind of our children. But who deserves that title? Us or God? Who is the only extraordinary parent? Us or God? Who is always consistent in their parenting? Us or God? Who never sins against their children? Us or God? Just think. God never has had to tell you, "I'm sorry for parenting you wrong." God has never had to repent to us for anything! God is the perfect parent and you have His manual (the Bible) to help you parent in this fallen dark world. Say with the psalmist, "Your word is a lamp to my feet and a light to my path" (Psalm 119:105). Let's look to the Creator of our hearts, the Author of parenthood and the Finisher. I'm reminded of a song that aptly describes grace. Words written by Julia Harriet Johnston (1849-1919) and music by Daniel Brink Towner.

Marvelous grace of our loving Lord,

grace that exceeds our sin and our guilt,

yonder on Calvary's mount outpoured,

there where the blood of the Lamb was spilt.

Grace, grace, God's grace,
grace that will pardon and cleanse within;
grace, grace, God's grace,
grace that is greater than all our sin.

Dark is the stain that we cannot hide,
what can avail to wash it away!
Look! there is flowing a crimson tide;
whiter than snow you may be today. [Refrain]

Marvelous, infinite, matchless grace,
freely bestowed on all who believe:
you that are longing to see his face,
will you this moment his grace receive?

Read Psalm 3 and psalm 40 for encouragement in your free time.

"The Lord bless you and keep you; the Lord make His face shine on you and be gracious to you; the Lord turn His face toward you and give you peace."

Numbers 6:24-26

⤞ WOUNDS ⤝

*N*ovember 24, 2019

The next time you have disconnect with your toddler or young child, try engaging in pretend play for just 15 minutes. But really be into it. And watch what happens. I tried this today and I think Eden opened about twenty band aids and put them all on a little white deer I bought her from Lowe's. Then she started saying "The Lord binds up our wounds." Amen to that. And we have many of them. We sure are a needy people. May He tend kindly to each of you reading this.

"He heals the brokenhearted, and binds up their wounds."

⟜Psalm 147:3

⋙ DOWNPOUR ⋘

"For to the snow he says, 'Fall on the earth,' likewise to the downpour, his mighty downpour."

⇒Job 37:6

November 25, 2019

We love Christmas time in Texas. We are praying for snow this year. Today seemed to be a record-breaking warm November day so....we made our own snow.

"For to the snow he says, 'Fall on the earth,' likewise to the downpour, his mighty downpour."

⇒Job 37:6

⊱ THANKSGIVING ⊰

"Oh give thanks to the Lord...call upon His name!"

⟲Psalm 105:1

𝒩*ovember 28, 2019*

HAPPY THANKSGIVING!

Rare family photo on Thanksgiving. I finally got him to snap a picture. Ha

"Oh give thanks to the Lord...call upon His name!"

⇒Psalm 105:1

☙ BIRTHDAY ❧

"Rejoice greatly, O daughter of Zion! Shout in triumph, O daughter of Jerusalem! Behold, your king is coming to you; He is just and endowed with salvation, Humble, and mounted on a donkey, Even on a colt, the foal of a donkey."

Zechariah 9:9

*D*ecember 14, 2019

Happy 3rd Birthday to Eden Joy!

Of all the cakes she wanted...she chose a bible cake.

"Rejoice greatly, O daughter of Zion! Shout in triumph, O daughter of Jerusalem! Behold, your king is coming to you; He is just and endowed with salvation, Humble, and mounted on a donkey, Even on a colt, the foal of a donkey."

—Zechariah 9:9

"Let Israel rejoice in their Maker; let the children of Zion rejoice in their King."

Psalm 149:2

*D*ecember 22, 2019

Merry merry CHRISTmas to you all.

May Christ be the center...of all your days.

Picture taken at our Christmas Church Service at Heritage Grace, Frisco, TX.

"Let Israel rejoice in their Maker; let the children of Zion rejoice in their King."

Psalm 149:2

❧ PRAYER ❧

*D*ecember 31, 2019

The best way to ring in the new year (in prayer!!)
Eden even made her dolls bow to God.

And speaking of Prayer, I'm praying she gets to work tomorrow on cleaning her kitchen when she wakes up. Ha

"Those who wait on the LORD will renew their strength."

Isaiah 40:31

"Trust in the LORD and do good; Dwell in the land and cultivate faithfulness."

⟩Psalm 37:3

*J*anuary 11, 2020

Eden prayed the most beautiful prayer just right now, "Lord help us to not fret, help us to not complain, help us to not fret and help us to obey in Jesus name, amen."

Good good prayer and reminder of this verse Psalm 37:8.

"Trust in the LORD and do good; Dwell in the land and cultivate faithfulness."

⟩Psalm 37:3

CHANGED

"To our God and Father be glory forever and ever. Amen."

Philippians 4:20

*J*anuary 12, 2020

Today my husband's life flashed before my eyes and how God brought him out of darkness and into the light.

Most people don't know that Emilio was a high school drop out and was deeply involved in a gang lifestyle and was living for himself and his own glory in Southern California and then God stepped in and blinded him (with a Saul like conversion) where God shed His marvelous light and all Emilio could do was cry for days and found himself later sitting in a Calvary Chapel where he listened for years to Chuck Smith teach verse by verse through the Bible and was baptized by him.

Emilio said his mind was so affected from his worldly lifestyle that he could not understand a single line of the Bible. And it took him months to get through and understand John 1:1 (just 1 verse!). And he purposed not to move on from that verse until he understood it.

And through a series of events, Emilio sensed a deep call of God to teach the Bible himself. And here we are today where he is the Pastor of HeritageGrace.com in Frisco, TX.

Come join us anytime for wonderful expositional verse by verse preaching.

And thank you (deeply) to Trent Douglass who poured into Emilio's life. Emilio is still reaping your labors.

Praise God's Name!!!!!

"To our God and Father be glory forever and ever. Amen."

Philippians 4:20

⤳ FAMILIES ⤳

"A man's heart plans his way, but the LORD directs his steps."

⟹Proverbs 16:9

*F*ebruary 7, 2020

Emilio thought I should become a realtor...

I laughed.

But I followed through (by faith) and God has done some wonderful things during the end of last year and last month in January.

Below are the families I helped and short stories of how God worked to bring it all together.

I was able to help five families into new homes in just under 4 months. Whew.

But don't worry. I have Eden as my assistant. My mom in the prayer division and Emilio as the driver and of course God is guiding it all.

Two families relocated from other states (to North Texas) and one family that was from out of the country!

The Nelson's were Wretched Radio listeners and that is how we met.

And Mike and Vanessa found us through listening to James R. White.

A total blessing!

Not sure if you can see in the pictures but Eden and I presented "As for me and my house we will serve the Lord" Joshua 24:15 signs to all our clients on closing day.

Nelson Family from Colorado

Mike and Vanessa from Arizona

Also Congratulations to Kristin and Mark from Canada on their brand new Texas home.

Kristin found me through one of my Facebook posts about me being a realtor.

When I connected with her on the phone, I found out she had listened to me a long time ago in the early days of The Way of the Master Radio. We talked and laughed and prayed, and the rest was history.

And...funny enough...they would buy a History Maker home.

It is after all HIS-STORY.

Mark and Kristin from Canada

Congratulations to Chris and Tere Gonzales on their brand new home!

Yes...! We even sell homes in the dark!!

Hahahah

I met Chris and Tere at a James White debate in Arlington, Texas about four years ago.

At the time they did not have a home church, but decided to make the LONG drive out to Frisco and visit Heritage Grace and have been with us ever since. They are real troupers.

After some house hunting, I found them the perfect home. Congratulations on that long drive coming to a close.

They are a precious family and I thank God for the day I met them. I never would've dreamed I'd be their realtor.

God works in mysterious ways.

Their daughter's name, Jubilee, means to "celebrate."

That's a perfect name for this occasion.

Gonzales Family

Closed in just 31 days!!!

The evening I showed Greg and Carianne and their son Noah several homes...this home (the one they are now standing in front of) was the first I was to show them.

And of all things there was a Ray Comfort Million Dollar Gospel tract on the fridge inside the home. I was amazed. Carianne looked at me as we stood in the kitchen and her jaw dropped.

I've been passing these tracts out for close to 20 years and Greg and his family have a while as well...it was the only thing on the entire fridge...

How kind of God to make the decision so easy for them. Ha

We asked the seller how he received it and he said his "sister mailed it to him."

And on Eden's bday (my clients didn't know this till today) I put the MLS listing of the home on our Christmas tree (before they chose it) so that my family and I could be in prayer over it.

To top it off my client (the buyer) presented a bible to the seller. What a deal to remember.

With God all things are possible. -Matt 19:26

Greg and Carianne

(Rare photo included....buyer (my clients Greg and Carianne), seller (right Mr. Bailey) AND both realtors (me the buyers realtor) and Jacqueline (sellers realtor) and my broker Ericka. So special.

Greg and Carianne's new home – lots of land.

"A man's heart plans his way, but the LORD directs his steps."

Proverbs 16:9

⤢ WORD OF THANKS ⤢

*F*ebruary 7-8, 2020

My utmost thanks to the Lord who helped bring this book together and who provided the dear people that got behind it.

Thank you to my mom who is always there for me (her only child). I am thankful that God called me to be her daughter and that He called her to be my only mom.

Thank you to Eden Joy. This past year has been full of adventures like Steven Curtis Chapman's song "Saddle up your horses we got a trail to blaze." Thank you for being such a fun and joyful person (exactly what your name means "Delightful Joy" and that you are)!

And thank you to John Manning for spending endless hours reading "Struggles and Sunshine" and laying it out so beautifully and now doing this same for this book "Next Steps". I thank God that he has given you the gift and time and energy and care to do this. You are valuable. May He give you many more years because this dark earth needs a great light like you.

Thank you to Chafi Charneco for the wonderful graphic work on "Struggles and Sunshine" and now this book. You are so gifted. Thank you for your service and I thank God for the day I met you almost a decade ago at a Ray Comfort and Living Waters event in Florida, your gift of graphics and your fast work has been such a help to me.

If you have read this far I want to personally thank you. If you've read this book and my first book I am blown away that you'd take the time to read and care about one person's story. God bless you for your time.

And for those reading this that are not Christians and do not know the Lord Jesus, trust in Him today. Just come to Him and confess your sin and error and trust in the finished work of Christ (who died on the cross for sinners and rose from the dead, defeating death and securing salvation for all who would repent and believe in Him – read John 3:16). Today is a fine day to trust in Him.

To all the moms reading this book, I look forward to hearing how God used this for your edification and growth and enjoyment, and since our time on earth is so short, you may have to tell me about it at the Marriage Supper of the Lamb.

Onward Christian mothers!

⤐ WORSHIP SONGS ⤏
BONUS FEATURE

My first book "Struggles and Sunshine" contained a Worship Bonus list too. Here are some new songs. Some oldies but goodies. And if you'd like a complete list you can find "Struggles and Sunshine" on Amazon. These are songs we would play and enjoy.

Songs with a fun beat and good words:

Paul Baloche

Because of Your Love

Big Daddy Weave

Alive

Overwhelmed

Seeds Family Worship

He is Faithful

Oldies from when I first got saved in late 90's:

Ron Kenoly

Ancient of Days

Brian Doerksen

Come, Now is the time to worship

Andy Park

River of God

Bob Fitts

I Can Do All Things

Ron Kenoly

Mourning Into Dancing

Sovereign Grace Kids (Awesome God CD)

Eden really enjoyed these two:

Almighty Creator

Jesus Came to Earth

Mercy Me CD (Almost There)

We played this CD over and over and over as Eden tumbled and played and did summersaults. She really loved the whole CD and especially the song called "In You". It's about how one day in heaven the lame will walk, the blind will see and the weary will find Rest in God.

Psalty (The Walking Bible from the 70's and 80's)

Eden was really into these Psalty songs late 2019 and early 2020, such fun!

Written in the Word (I especially like the words on this song)

Psalty's Songs for Lil Praisers (all volumes)

Chris Tomlin

Where the Spirit of the Lord is There is Liberty

God of Angel Armies

Steven Curtis Chapman

Saddle up your Horses

☙ ALSO BY TRISH RAMOS ❧

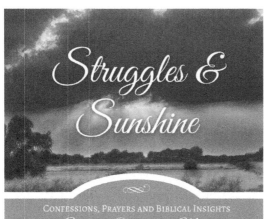

Available on Amazon